Planning Focus Groups

David L. Morgan
with Alice U. Scannell

Planning Focus Groups

Focus Group Kit2

SAGE Publications
International Educational and Professional Publisher
Thousand Oaks   London   New Delhi

For information:

 SAGE Publications, Inc.
2455 Teller Road
Thousand Oaks, California 91320
E-mail: order@sagepub.com

SAGE Publications Ltd.
6 Bonhill Street
London EC2A 4PU
United Kingdom

SAGE Publications India Pvt. Ltd.
M-32 Market
Greater Kailash I
New Delhi 110 048 India

Printed in the United States of America

Library of Congress Cataloging-in-Publication Data

Morgan, David L., Krueger, Richard A.
    The focus group kit.
        p.   cm.
    Includes bibliographical references and indexes.
    Contents: v. 1. The focus group guidebook/David L. Morgan.   v. 2. Planning focus groups/David L. Morgan.   v. 3. Developing questions for focus groups/Richard A. Krueger. v. 4. Moderating focus groups/Richard A. Krueger.   v. 5. Involving community members in focus groups/Richard A. Krueger, Jean A. King.   v. 6. Analyzing and reporting focus group results/Richard A. Krueger.

ISBN 0-7619-0760-2 (pbk.: The focus group kit: alk. paper)

1. Focus groups.   I. Title.   II. Series.   III. Morgan, David L.   IV. Krueger, Richard A.

H61.28K778 1997
001.4'33—dc21   97-21135

ISBN 0-7619-0818-8 (v. 1 pbk.)
ISBN 0-7619-0817-X (v. 2 pbk.)
ISBN 0-7619-0819-6 (v. 3 pbk.)
ISBN 0-7619-0821-8 (v. 4 pbk.)
ISBN 0-7619-0820-X (v. 5 pbk.)
ISBN 0-7619-0816-1 (v. 6 pbk.)

This book is printed on acid-free paper.

99 00 01 02 03 10 9 8 7 6 5 4

Acquiring Editor:	Marquita Flemming
Editorial Assistant:	Frances Borghi
Production Editor:	Diana E. Axelsen
Production Assistant:	Karen Wiley
Typesetter/Designer:	Janelle LeMaster
Cover Designer:	Ravi Balasuriya
Cover Illustration:	Anahid Moradkhan
Print Buyer:	Anna Chin

Brief Table
of Contents

Detailed Table
of Contents

Acknowledgments

I want to start by thanking my coauthor, Alice Scannell, who wrote the essential first drafts for Chapters 3 and 4. Alice also conducted several interviews with colleagues who helped expand our understanding of how people use focus groups, including Bruce Bayley, of the Center for Outcomes Rsearch and Education at Providence Medical Center; Adam Davis, of Davis and Hibbitts Incorporated; and Laura Neidhart, of Bardsley and Neidhart. Bruce provided insights into the concerns of those who contract with others for focus groups. Laura shared her knowledge of various aspects of the focus group industry, including the role that professional focus group facilities play. And Adam helped us understand the issues that professional focus group researchers encounter when working for others.

I would also like to acknowledge the numerous students and colleagues whose focus group projects I have been a part of. Some of what is here is indeed my own hard-won experience about how to plan for effective focus groups. I have learned at least as much, however, by sharing in the wide range of uses that my students and colleagues have found for focus groups.

Introduction to the Focus Group Kit

We welcome you to this series of books on focus group interviewing. We hope that you find this series helpful. In this section, we would like to tell you a bit about our past work with focus groups, the factors that led to the creation of this series, and an overview of how the book is organized.

We began our studies of focus group interviewing about the same time. Our academic backgrounds were different (David in sociology and Richard in program evaluation) and yet we were both drawn to focus group interviewing in the 1980s. We both had books published in 1988 on focus group interviewing that resulted from your research and practice with the methodology. At that time we were unaware of one another's work and were pleased to begin a collegial relationship. Over the years we've continued our studies independently, and occasionally our paths crossed and we had an opportunity to work together. In the last decade, we've worked together in writing articles, sharing advice on research studies, and teaching classes. We have generally found that we shared many common thoughts and concerns about focus group interviewing.

During the 1990s, we found that interest in focus groups continued and we both prepared second editions for our 1988 books. In 1995, the staff at Sage Publications asked us to consider developing a more in-depth treatment of focus group interviewing that would allow for more detail and guide researchers beyond the basic issues. We pondered the request and thought about how the materials might be presented. We weighed a variety of options and finally developed the kit in its present form. We developed this kit in an effort to help guide both novices and experts.

In these books the authors have occasionally chosen to use the word *we*. Although the authors share many common experiences with focus groups, our approaches can and do vary, as we hope is the case with other researchers as well. When you see the word *we* in the books of this series, it typically refers to a judgment decision by the specific author(s) of that particular volume. Much of what the authors have learned about focus groups has been acquired, absorbed, and assimilated from the experiences of others. We use *we* in circumstances where one of us personally has experienced a situation that has been verified by another researcher or when a practice or behavior has become standard accepted practice by a body of focus group moderators. The use of *I,* on the other hand, tends to refer to situations and experiences that one of us has witnessed that may not have been verified by other researchers.

In terms of content, we decided on six volumes, each representing a separate theme. The volumes include the following:

- **Volume 1:** *The Focus Group Guidebook*

This volume provides a general introduction to focus group research. The central topics are the appropriate reasons for using focus groups and what you can expect to accomplish with them. This book is intended to help those who are new to focus groups.

- **Volume 2:** *Planning Focus Groups*

This volume covers the wide range of practical tasks that need to get done in the course of a research project using focus groups. A major topic is making the basic decisions about the group's format, such as the size of the groups, their composition, the total number of groups, and so forth.

- **Volume 3:** *Developing Questions for Focus Groups*

This book describes a practical process for identifying powerful themes and then offers an easy-to-understand strategy for translating those themes into questions. This book helps make the process of developing good questions doable by outlining a process and offering lots of examples.

- **Volume 4:** *Moderating Focus Groups*

The book is an overview of critical skills needed by moderators, the various approaches that successful moderators use, and strategies for handling difficult situations. Rookie moderators will find this book to be an invaluable guide and veteran moderators will discover tips and strategies for honing their skills.

- **Volume 5:** *Involving Community Members in Focus Groups*

This book is intended for those who want to teach others to conduct focus group interviews, particularly non-researchers in communities. Volunteers can often gather and present results more effectively than professionals. A critical element is how the volunteers are prepared and the manner in which they work together.

- **Volume 6:** *Analyzing and Reporting Focus Group Results*

Analysis of focus group data is different from analysis of data collected through other qualitative methodologies and this presents new challenges to researchers. This book offers an overview of important principles guiding focus group research and then suggests a systematic and verifiable analysis strategy.

Early on we struggled with how these materials might be presented. In order to help you find your way around the series, we developed several strategies. First, we are providing an expanded table of contents and an overview of topics at the beginning of each chapter. These elements help the reader quickly grasp the overall picture and understand the relationship between specific sections. Second, we've attempted to make the indexes as useful as possible. Volumes 2-6 contain two indexes: an index for that volume and a series index to help you find your way around the entire kit of six books. Finally, we are using icons to identify materials of interest. These icons serve several purposes. Some icons help you locate other materials within the series that amplify a particular topic. Other icons expand on a particular point, share a story or tip, or provide background material not included in the text. We like the icons because they have allowed us to expand on certain points without interrupting the flow of the discussion. The icons have also allowed us to incorporate the wisdom of other focus group experts. We hope you find them beneficial. We've also included icons in the book to help you discover points of interest.

The **BACKGROUND** icon identifies the bigger picture and places the current discussion into a broader context.

The **CAUTION** icon highlights an area where you should be careful. These are especially intended to help beginners spot potholes or potential roadblocks.

The **CHECKLIST** icon identifies a list of items that are good to think about; they may or may not be in a sequence.

The **EXAMPLE** icon highlights stories and illustrations of general principles.

The **EXERCISE** icon suggests something you could do to practice and improve your skills, or something you could suggest to others to help them improve their skills.

The **GO TO** icon is a reference to a specific place in this book or one of the other volumes where you will find additional discussion of the topic.

The **KEY POINT** icon identifies the most important things in each section. Readers should pay attention to these when skimming a section for the first time or reviewing it later.

The **TIP** icon highlights a good practice to follow or something that has successfully worked for us.

We hope you find this series helpful and interesting.

—Richard A. Krueger
St. Paul, Minnesota

—David L. Morgan
Portland, Oregon

1

About This Book

The essence of planning is making good decisions. Although we could give this decision-making process a more elevated tone by calling it "research design," the emphasis throughout this volume will be on the practical choices that are necessary for focus group research.

Awareness is the crucial prerequisite to good decision making, so each chapter in this book raises issues that require decisions. For those who are new to focus groups, this material will alert you to the decisions that need to be made. For those with more experience, reencountering these necessary decisions may help you question some of your assumptions.

Once you are aware that a decision has to be made, you need to know what the options are. There are many different ways of doing focus groups, and most of the material in this volume is a summary of these options. Throughout, there is an emphasis on matching different options to different purposes. Knowing what you want to accomplish is the key to deciding among the available options.

Chapters 2 through 4 provide an overview of the issues that affect the planning process. If a journey of a thousand miles begins with but a single step, then it is crucial to take that first step in the right direction. Think of a project using focus groups as such a journey. The time you spend planning and preparing not only ensures that you arrive at your intended destination, but also gets you there with a minimum of wasted time and effort.

After Chapter 2's summary of guiding principles of planning, Chapters 3 and 4 present extended examples of the timelines, budgets, and personnel associated with focus group projects. Taken together, these initial chapters consider the full set of planning decisions that go into a focus group project, while the later chapters examine the separate decisions that make up the planning process. In practice, however, those separate decisions will work only if they are well integrated. This volume thus begins by considering the planning process as a whole.

Chapters 5 through 8 present the more specific decisions that need to be made in the course of planning a research project using focus groups. Chapter 5 examines choices about the degree of structure that the interview questions and moderator impose on the group discussion. Chapter 6 presents the options associated with selecting the composition of the groups. Chapter 7 reviews the issues involved in deciding on group size. Chapter 8 examines the factors that determine the number of groups that are necessary. Each of these specific decisions needs to be thought through during the planning process. Putting conscious effort into these decisions helps ensure the quality of the overall results from your work.

The last three chapters go over the actual planning issues involved in setting up focus group sessions. Chapter 9 covers the realities of recruitment. The fact that this is the longest chapter in the book signals not only the detailed planning that needs to go into recruitment but also the broader importance of recruitment to the success of the project as a whole. Chapter 10 discusses how to select and set up locations for the sessions. Chapter 11 concludes the volume by reviewing the fundamental decisions that need to made throughout the planning process.

Throughout, each of these chapters will emphasize a basic set of principles:

- The success of the project at every stage depends on planning.
- Effective planning consists of comparing options and making decisions.
- Good decisions require a clear sense of your goals and purposes.

Planning is thus more than a mechanical set of procedures. It is, ultimately, a matter of deciding what you want to accomplish and how you will do it.

2

Guiding Principles of Planning

Overview

Think Through the Project From Start to Finish
Four Basic Steps
Plan to Meet Your Purposes:
"It All Depends on What You Want"
Planning: The Big Picture

The groups themselves are the most obvious part of any focus group project. Yet, in many ways, these groups are just the proverbial "tip of the iceberg." At a minimum, a successful set of groups depends on careful preparation. Furthermore, a successful project depends on more than just conducting good groups. After all, the real issue is what you do with the data that the groups provide.

We thus do not think of the planning process as something that happens up front. Instead, we emphasize a planning process that carries through from the first decision to use focus groups to the final analysis and reporting.

Think Through the Project From Start to Finish

The key to planning in focus groups is to think through the whole project. Those who are new to focus groups too often think solely in terms of the group discussions themselves. Those with more experience pay just as much attention to the work that occurs before and after the actual groups. What needs to be planned is the complete research project, not just moderating the focus groups themselves.

KEY POINT

What Needs to Be Planned Is the Complete Research Project

Fortunately, thinking through the project as a whole is not as difficult as it may sound, even if this is your first time using focus groups. Virtually all research projects using focus groups consist of four basic steps:

- Planning
- Recruiting
- Moderating
- Analyzing and reporting

Thinking through these steps will help you plan for the project as a whole.

Four Basic Steps

Planning

Successful projects begin with careful planning. The goal in this step is to anticipate the major decisions that need to be made. This volume is dedicated to helping you make smart choices associated with the many planning decisions that are necessary for a successful project. In addition to the general discussion in this volume, three of the most crucial concerns in the planning process each receive extended coverage in this kit.

GO TO

See *Developing Questions for Focus Groups, Moderating Focus Groups,* and *Analyzing and Reporting Focus Group Results*

Recruiting

Having the right participants in the groups is every bit as important as asking good questions or using a skilled moderator. Although recruitment may be one of the more mundane steps in a focus group project, it is absolutely essential. Problems with recruitment are the single most common reason why things go wrong in focus group projects, so solid recruitment planning is one of the smartest moves you can make.

Moderating

When most people think about focus groups, they think about moderating. Taking part in the participants' discussions is undoubtedly the most exciting part of the process. After all, these discussions are the data! But effective discussions don't happen magically. At a minimum, you need to have good questions and successful recruitment. It is this prior planning that makes good moderating possible.

Analysis and Reporting

There is little point in gathering high-quality data if you don't use them well. Failing to plan for the analysis can result in either of two very different problems. Sometimes, the amount or complexity of the data is overwhelming, and the analysis consists of little more than grabbing a few high points. At the other extreme, sometimes too much effort goes into combing through materials that really don't matter. By planning what needs to be in the final report, you can avoid the trap of either underanalyzing or overanalyzing the data.

Taking all four of these steps into account, the fundamental message is that moderating is just the tip of the iceberg. In most focus group projects, the time that is spent actually moderating groups is less than the time spent on each of the other three basic steps—often far less. Yes, moderating is a crucial step, but no more so than the other three. If you don't ask the right questions, or talk to the right people, or know what to do with the data, then it doesn't matter how good a job the moderator does. A successful focus group project requires careful attention to all of these concerns.

Plan to Meet Your Purposes: "It All Depends on What You Want"

There is an old adage in farming: If you want to plow a straight row, you need to set your sights on the end of the field. If instead you look down and just think where you are going from step to step, you're more likely to stumble and wander. Likewise, a clear goal is the single most essential element in planning focus groups. So, aim at where you want to be when you finish, and you'll be more likely to follow a straight path to that goal.

TIP

Aim at Where You Want to Be

If there are several different ways to accomplish something, how do you know which is the best? The answer is that it depends on the project's goals. Making effective decisions requires knowing what the project is supposed to accomplish. This leads to a simple test for every decision: Does this choice help to meet the project's goals? As the chapters in this volume demonstrate, much of the planning in focus groups consists of asking questions such as the following:

- Can the project be done in-house, or does it require outside experts?
- Who should the participants be, and what will it take to recruit them?
- Will these discussions work better with larger groups or smaller ones?
- Does this project need more groups, or can it get by with fewer?
- Will an oral report be sufficient, or is a more thorough report needed?

Evaluating the advantages and disadvantages of these different options is impossible without knowing what kind of purposes the project is supposed to serve. If you don't know where you're going, it doesn't matter how you get there.

EXERCISE

Experiencing Different Goals

Take a minute to imagine two different projects that you might actually do using focus groups.

First, think of a project where what you want to learn is relatively clear-cut. In this kind of explanatory research, you know what the questions are, and you simply need to hear the answers.

Second, think of a project where you are much less certain of what you need to know. In this kind of exploratory research, you are often trying to learn what the right questions are.

Once you've thought of a realistic example for each of these two different types of projects, ask yourself if both of these projects should be done the same way?

- *Would you talk to the same types of participants?*
- *Would you ask the same kinds of questions in your interviews?*
- *Would you produce the same kinds of reports?*

Chance are, you'll conclude that meeting such different goals would require different approaches.

All of this talk about goals can seem very abstract when a project is just beginning. One of the most effective ways to think about the project's goals is to plan ahead for the final report (or oral presentation, journal article, etc.).

Right from the start, be as specific as possible in defining the ultimate products from the project and the purposes that these products will serve. This means thinking about the audience for the final report. What will be important to them? How will they judge whether the research was done well? The final report is frequently the point at which your research does or doesn't make a difference. Begin the project by planning for a final report that really will make a difference.

Start by Thinking About the Final Report

Planning: The Big Picture

The next two chapters will consider "big-picture" issues:

- Timelines: What is the schedule for the steps in the project?
- Personnel and budgeting: What resources are necessary at each step?

These big-picture issues affect the specific decisions that occur at every stage in the research. Each choice you make will be influenced by the timelines, personnel, and budget associated with the project as a whole.

3

Planning and Timelines

This chapter presents the essential issues in planning a timeline for a focus group project. Each of the four basic steps—planning, recruiting, moderating, and analyzing and reporting—needs its own planning process and timeline. This chapter thus begins with an overview of the basic decisions that occur within each of these four steps. This overview provides a purposely brief introduction to the decisions that go into a focus group project. Next, we present examples of the planning process for both a smaller and a larger focus group project, since the size and scope of a project are the primary factors that affect planning and timelines. Finally, we consider some of the specific factors that can shorten or lengthen a project timeline.

Planning

Although planning and decision making continue throughout any project, the explicit planning stage occurs at the beginning. Consequently, much of the work that is done up front consists of identifying the issues that must be confronted during the project as a whole. The basic decisions in the planning process are the following:

- Define the purpose and outcomes of the project
- Identify the role of the sponsor in the project
- Identify personnel and staffing resources
- Develop the timeline for the project
- Determine who the participants will be
- Write the questions in the interview guide
- Develop a recruitment plan
- Set the locations, dates, and time for the sessions
- Design the analysis plan
- Specify the elements of the final report

The timeline for the planning process can vary considerably, depending on both the size of the project and the research team's experience. Often, the best way to determine how difficult the planning process will be is to draft a preliminary timeline. If planning this timeline is a straightforward task, then the rest of the planning process is likely to be equally straightforward. If, however, it is not obvious what needs to be done when, then setting aside more planning time may well be an "ounce of prevention" that takes the place of a subsequent "pound of cure."

Be Generous With Planning Time

One crucial concern in the planning stage is to allow enough time for thoughtful discussions between the sponsor and the research team. The foremost decisions that the sponsor will need to approve are the project's goals, the resources to commit, the questions for the discussion guide, and the desired final product(s). Depending on the nature of the project, the sponsor may also need to approve the recruitment plan, the choice of a moderator, the location for the group sessions, and any external stimulus materials (e.g., sample designs for brochures or posters) that you will use in the discussion. Hence, the sponsor and the research team need a clear understanding of each other's roles and responsibilities, right from the start.

Recruiting

Recruiting is one of the most important aspects of the planning process. There is nothing more frustrating and embarrassing than to go through all the effort to put together a focus group and have only three people show up. It is thus imperative to devote sufficient time and effort to recruitment, even for small projects. The specific tasks during the recruitment phase are the following:

- Define the target population
- Define segments within the target population
- Identify the appropriate composition for each group
- Develop eligibility and exclusion criteria for individual participants
- Develop recruitment screening and invitation scripts
- Make the initial recruitment contacts with potential participants
- Determine the follow-up procedures that will ensure attendance

The timeline for recruitment often has a dominant influence on the timeline for the entire project. In particular, the length of time that it takes to put together a group determines when the data collection can begin. As a general rule, the recruitment contacts for each group should begin at least two weeks before that group. This allows time not only to locate participants, but also to send each participant a confirmation letter, map, and other materials. In essence, recruitment is still going on the day before each session, as you make calls to remind each participant to attend.

Chapter 9 Has More Information on Recruiting

Moderating

The role of the moderator in the planning process varies. Often the moderator is also the primary researcher who works with the sponsor to design the project from the beginning. Other times the moderator is brought in at a later point for the sole purpose of facilitating the focus group discussions. The basic decisions associated with moderating are as follows:

- Define the role of the moderator
- Decide if multiple moderators will be needed for the project
- Either train moderators or select skilled moderators
- Develop the questions for the discussion guide
- Identify external props or materials that will be used in the sessions

- Clarify the sponsor's involvement at the focus group sessions
- Clarify the arrangements for the location, recording equipment, and so forth
- Determine what kinds of field notes the moderator will generate

The most obvious part of the timeline for moderating is the two hours spent in leading a group. Yet, even when the moderator is hired expressly for this limited role, his or her rsponsibilities extend beyond the actual moderation. Prior to the groups, the moderator needs to understand what the goals of the projects are, who the participants are, and why the interview guide is written in the way that it is. If possible, the moderator should take part in drafting the interview guide. After each group, the moderator needs to contribute his or her observations in the debriefing session. Moderators themselves are also a source of data, not just a means for producing data!

Analysis

Planning for the analysis phase takes into account the scope and purpose of the project as well as the reporting of results to the project's sponsor. Even a simple project can produce a great deal of data that must be sorted, understood, interpreted, and summarized. The basic tasks related to analysis are the following:

- Estimate the amount of time devoted to analysis
- Organize the field notes, tapes, transcripts, and other data
- Study the data to determine the key conclusions
- Organize the products of the analysis to match the format of the final report
- Prepare the final report
- Meet with the sponsor to report the results of the project

Estimating the timeline for analysis is one of the more difficult aspects of planning. The time devoted to analysis can be highly variable, depending on the complexity of the issues you are addressing and the nature of the final report. For most projects, the analysis begins with either writing field notes or holding debriefing sessions following each group. For the simplest projects, the field notes and/or post-group debriefings will be the sole basis for the final report. More often, the analysis will involve reviewing the contents of each group while either listening to the tape or reading a transcript.

The time involved in writing and presenting the report itself is strictly a function of what the sponsor requests. The report could be of several types: written only, oral only, or both written and oral. The preparation of any written record of the analysis requires care, since it may be widely disseminated or otherwise acquire a life of its own. Adding even a short executive summary to accompany an oral report is not a trivial request.

Analyzing and Reporting Focus Group Results
Discusses Formats for Reports

Planning and Timelines for Smaller Focus Group Projects

The importance of good planning does not decrease just because a project is relatively small. Granted, the level of effort and the nature of the planning for a smaller project is not the same as in a larger project. Still, regardless of the size of the project, producing quality results depends on effective prior planning. When a smaller set of focus groups is a component within a larger project, the planning process is especially important, because the outcome of the larger enterprise may depend on success in the small project.

Characteristics of a Typical Smaller Focus Group Project

- *Two to four groups*
- *Most of the work done in-house by the sponsor's staff*
- *Easily available recruitment source(s) for the focus group participants*
- *Does not require complex analysis or full transcription of tapes*
- *Produces a brief report, such as an executive summary and an oral presentation*

BACKGROUND

Characteristics of a Typical Smaller Focus Group Project

Any given smaller project may not match all of these criteria. For example, a smaller project might involve six groups, if you can recruit the participants easily. Or you might bring in an outside consultant on a smaller project, if there is someone who is quite familiar with your needs. One or two such shifts toward greater complexity may not make much difference, but each of them has to be carefully thought out as part of the planning process. Some changes do make a considerable difference. For example, a project that involves a major report on even as few as four groups may require much more work than what we will describe in this section.

EXAMPLE

Examples of Smaller Focus Group Projects

Examples of Smaller Focus Group Projects

- *A magazine holds focus groups to get reactions to several possible new designs for its format prior to concentrating on the two most likely ones.*
- *A statewide organization ends its annual conference with a series of focus groups to plan for next year's conference.*
- *A political candidate uses focus groups among potential grassroots workers to understand the factors that would motivate them to help with her campaign.*
- *A student working on a master's degree conducts focus groups with new residents of a rapidly growing suburb to learn their reasons for moving there.*
- *A large volunteer organization conducts focus groups with its members to help design a survey questionnaire about preferences for new programs.*

As an example of the specific decisions that go into the timeline for a smaller project, assume that you are conducting an in-house project using focus groups to gather feedback from the users of your service, program, or product. Your existing information will make it relatively easy to locate enough participants for four groups. You have one staff person who has some experience with focus group research, and you are able to have that person spend most of his or her time on the project until it is completed. Staff from your office will do the recruitment; make arrangements for a place to hold the group; analyze the data; and both write and present the report of the findings. You want to complete the whole project within 6 weeks. What kind of time will you need for planning? Recruitment? Moderating the groups? Analysis and reporting?

Here is a potential timeline for such a project.

EXAMPLE

Generic Timeline for Smaller Focus Group Projects

Week:	1	2	3	4	5	6
Planning	▓▓	▓				
Recruiting		▓	▓	▓		
Moderating				▓		
Analysis				▓	▓	▓

Although such timelines will usually follow a predictable, linear sequence, the stages often overlap. For example, this timeline assumes that you can start recruitment while you are wrapping up other aspects of the planning process, such as writing the interview guide. Recruitment and moderating also overlap, since you will be making reminder calls for the later groups while the first ones are going on. Finally, because the sessions are spread over a period of several days, this timeline assumes that you will start analyzing data from the earlier groups before the later groups are completed.

The explicit planning process is concentrated in the first 2 weeks of the project. Because the recruitment is scheduled to begin in the second week, the decisions that affect recruitment will be among the first that you make. Who will the participants be? How will they be located and contacted? Who will do the recruiting? What will be the "script" for the recruitment contacts between the project staff and the potential participants? In addition, it will be necessary to determine when and where the groups will be held, because this information has to be given to the participants during the recruitment phase. In other words, a great many logistical decisions have to be made fairly quickly. The subsequent planning time will be devoted primarily to writing the interview guide and preparing the moderating team.

Recruitment for a project such as this would typically consist of making phone calls to potential participants. This generic timeline assumes a 2-week lead time from when phone calls begin to the first focus group. This is based on how long it will probably take to find the necessary number of willing participants for each group and to mail them a confirmation letter. For the present purposes, we are assuming that the recruitment will use a ready-made list of potential participants (e.g., employees, members of an organization, past clients or customers, and so forth). These contact calls continue through the end of Week 3 to set up the final focus groups in the following week. Recruiting ends with reminder calls just before each group, which the timeline shows as two discrete pieces of recruitment effort during Week 4.

A total of one week is devoted to moderating the four focus groups themselves. This timing takes into account the limits on not only the moderator's capacity but also the participants' schedules. With regard to the moderator, even a seasoned professional would find it unwise to schedule more than two groups per day, since too many groups in a short time fatigues the moderator and adversely affects the quality of the data. Even if the moderator could accommodate cramming all four groups into 2 days, the participants' schedules might not make this practical. A week is often a more realistic span for collecting this amount of data.

Analysis and reporting receive 2½ weeks in this timeline, with approximately 2 weeks devoted solely to analysis. The fact that the beginning of the analysis coincides with conducting the focus groups reflects an assumption that the moderator will generate either field notes or debriefing sessions after each group. Some moderators prefer to work alone and write up their field notes immediately following each session. Others prefer to bring along an assistant or members of the sponsoring organization and hold a debriefing discussion following each group.

Once the groups are complete, the principal analysis activity consists of a review of the tape from each group. Making notes from a tape usually takes at least twice as long as the time on the tape itself, because you will need to pause and rewind the tape at certain places to note something important or jot down quotations. Finally, the analyses from each of the separate groups are pulled together into an integrated report for the project as a whole. For this smaller project, we have assumed that the report will consist of a brief executive summary that is distributed and discussed at an oral presentation lasting about an hour. This presentation marks the end of the project.

Planning and Timelines for Larger Focus Group Projects

Larger focus group projects are distinguished by their complexity, with more groups, more variation in group composition and/or geographical location, more demanding analysis requirements, and greater reporting commitments. A larger focus group project will usually have several of the following characteristics:

BACKGROUND

Characteristics of a Typical Larger Focus Group Project

Characteristics of a Typical Smaller Focus Group Project

- *At least four groups*
- *Multiple staff, possibly including outside experts*
- *No ready-made recruitment source*
- *Recruitment across several segments or geographic locations*
- *Detailed data analysis, possibly requiring full transcription of tapes*
- *An extensive, written report plus an oral report with questions and answers*

Any one of these characteristics may be enough to shift an otherwise small project into a more complex planning process and a longer time frame. For example, if even three or four groups must be conducted in widely scattered locations, this can greatly complicate the logistics. Similarly, what might otherwise be an in-house project may require additional effort if the recruitment process is demanding.

- *A county social service agency has concentrated on expanding its services to several ethnic minority groups by developing a series of culturally sensitive services. The agency contracts with a consultant to evaluate the success of its efforts by conducting focus groups with each of the three largest ethnic minority groups in the area.*

- *A candidate for state political office has been selected in the primary election. She contracts for a series of focus groups to test how voters perceive her and her opponent, concentrating on what they think are the two candidates' most desirable and undesirable characteristics. She is particularly interested in the perceptions of voters from the following segments: male versus female, urban versus rural versus suburban, and members of her own party versus "swing" voters. The results will help her develop her campaign strategy and promotional materials.*

- *A beer manufacturer conducts focus groups to investigate how younger drinkers will respond to a new line of full-flavored beers, similar to those produced by microbreweries. The manufacturer wants to explore what segments exist in this target market and what types of packaging and advertising strategies appeal to each of these segments.*

- *A state university system, with several separate campuses, decides to conduct focus groups as part of its efforts to develop a new strategic plan and mission statement. They hire a consultant who will conduct interviews in rural, suburban, and metropolitan areas of the state with a variety of stakeholders, including current students, parents of current students, and representatives from business and industry. The major purpose of the groups is to explore regional and stakeholder differences in beliefs about the mission of higher education. In addition, they wish to test responses to the idea of having specialized services and programs at specific campuses rather than "all-purpose" education at each campus.*

- *A federal agency is interested in finding out the extent to which baby boomers are saving for retirement and doing economic planning for their later years. Focus groups will be held in several regions of the country, and the groups in each location will be divided into separate segments according to income and two-earner versus single-earner families. The research will examine the differences between those who save and those who do not, as well as the kind of messages that would encourage the non-savers to begin setting aside money for retirement.*

EXAMPLE

Examples of Larger Focus Group Projects

As an example of the specific decisions that go into the timeline for a larger project, assume that your project requires data from multiple segments in each of several geographic areas. To be more explicit, assume that you want to hear from both users and nonusers of your service, program, or product at each of four locations, for a total of eight groups. You will hire both a firm to do the recruitment services and a professional moderator to conduct the groups. The moderator, along with his or her research assistants, will perform the analysis. The ultimate product from the research will be a detailed report, which will be reviewed and revised prior to its final acceptance.

Here is a potential timeline for a larger project such as this.

EXAMPLE

Generic Timeline for Larger Focus Group Projects

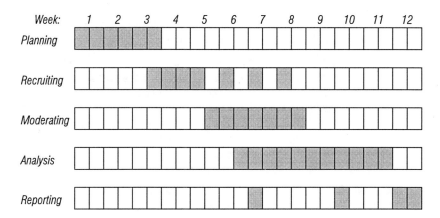

Compared to the smaller project, the time allocated to the planning process has been lengthened to 3 weeks. This reflects not only the more complicated logistics associated with this multi-site project but also the time necessary to select the professional recruiter(s) and moderator(s). For our purposes, we will assume that the project hires a single moderator who will travel to each of the four sites.

The recruitment timeline is directly affected by this decision to use a single moderator who travels to different locations, because the recruitment at each site will have to begin approximately 2 weeks prior to the groups at each location. As with the smaller project, recruitment is a three-part process consisting of an initial contact to find a participant, a follow-up mailing, and a reminder call immediately before the session.

The most obvious factor that lengthens the moderating phase is the time that it takes to travel to each location. Travel time could include the moderator's arrival the day before the group in order to check local arrangements involving the recruitment and the locations for the groups. Experience tells us that something unexpected often happens that requires on-site "fixing" before participants arrive for the focus group. The timeline here assumes that the pair of groups at each location can be done in either a single day or 2 days at the most.

The time needed for analysis of a large project is significantly longer than for a smaller project. Detailed analysis of these data will be based on transcriptions of audiotapes. The analysis is set to begin somewhat after the first set of groups, to allow time for transcription of those tapes. A typical strategy for such an analysis might first capture the key themes from each group and then make comparisons between the themes that occur both in groups of users versus nonusers and between groups from different locations.

We have concluded this timeline by listing reporting as a separate activity. Given the greater effort and expense in a larger project such as this, there is considerably more attention to reporting than in a smaller project. Here, we have built in three reporting sessions, starting with a preliminary "midstream" report while the groups are still being conducted. This gives the sponsor a chance to react to what the moderator is learning, thus sharpening the moderator's sense of what the sponsor needs from the remaining groups. The second reporting session, in Week 10, involves the presentation of a preliminary version of the report. This report should be able to stand as a final product, if it is accepted without revisions. In this case, however, we have built in an assumption of revisions. For example, this could be the first time that this sponsor has worked with either this topic or this target audience, so there may well be additional requests, once the sponsor's representatives read the initial version of the report. The timeline thus includes additional analysis time leading up to the final delivery of the revised report.

If the sponsor requests recommendations, be sure to allocate additional time. Explicit recommendations that guide future actions, decisions, or policies are not automatically included in a focus group report. Some sponsors are merely interested in a summary of findings. If a sponsor truly wants advice on what to do next, this will typically require additional meetings between members of the research team and the sponsoring organization.

The point of this extra time and effort is to understand the specific findings of the focus groups within a broader context that includes organizational history and culture, resources and limitations, policy and procedures, and so on. Taking all of this into account will almost surely make the writing of the report more complex, but it is virtually impossible to produce meaningful recommendations without this additional work.

Requests for Recommendations Require Special Care

Factors That Can Shorten or Lengthen a Focus Group Project

This final section goes beyond the basic distinction between larger and smaller projects to consider some of the specific factors that can either shorten or lengthen a project timeline. We will once again divide this presentation into the four stages of planning, recruitment, moderating, and analysis.

Planning

This stage will go faster if the purpose of the research has been well specified. Do the sponsor and the researcher already have a clear consensus about the goals of the research, who they want to talk with, the questions they want to ask, and the format for the final report? If so, the planning process will be shorter.

The number of people working on a project is one of the more obvious factors that affects the amount of time it will take. There is, however, no simple relationship between staff size and the project timeline. At one extreme, a project can take longer if only one person takes care of all the planning, recruiting, moderating, analysis, and reporting. At the other extreme, the complexities of coordinating a large staff can also take more time.

Prior experience with focus groups also has a major influence on planning and timelines. It helps if an experienced research team is conducting the project. Allow more time if those doing the recruitment, moderating, and analysis have not conducted at least two successful focus group projects.

Sponsors also affect timing. When there is a committee and task force in charge of the project, decision making can be quite slow. Having one person in charge of decisions will speed up the process, especially when it comes to finalizing the interview questions. Things will also go more quickly if the project sponsor has used focus groups successfully in the past and understands the process involved.

Recruiting

The most important factor that will shorten the recruitment stage is immediate access to a well-defined group of eligible participants, such as employees, members of an organization, and clients or customers. The timeline will be lengthened if recruitment consists of "cold calls" that screen members of the general public into the participant pool according to various eligibility criteria, such as age, education, sex, prior experience and with a product or service.

The difficulty of recruitment is also a function of who the desired participants are and where they are. More time and more planning will be necessary when the participants that you are seeking are rare, hard to locate, or difficult to schedule. Recruitment will also go more slowly when the contacts are either nonlocal or dispersed over several geographical areas. It will also take longer to recruit participants who do not have some prior commitment to the study. In any of these circumstances, the availability of a prequalified list of potential participants will make a tremendous difference.

Recruitment is also easier when the target audience has an inherent interest in participating in focus groups, since this minimizes turn-downs. The planning process should thus consider the incentives that will appeal to participants. As Chapter 9 of this book makes clear, these incentives are not limited to offering cash payments. As a more general rule, your planning efforts should ensure that your recruitment pitch appeals to peoples' preexisting motivations for participating.

Finally, you can sometimes shorten the recruitment time by using a professional recruiting service. If you are willing to pay for more of their staff to work on your project, they will be able to make the necessary recruitment contacts within a short period.

Moderating

If you have more than one moderator, you will be able to conduct groups simultaneously or very close together. Multiple moderators also make it much easier to operate at several locations. Even when only two moderators are available, tighter scheduling is possible when they alternate the roles of moderator and assistant, allowing for two or more groups per day. There is, however, a cost to using multiple moderators, since you will need to invest more time in analysis, compared with having a single person both conduct all of the groups and do the analysis.

One possible substitute for the time savings associated with multiple moderators is a single, highly experienced facilitator. These professionals may be able to do either multiple groups per day or groups at remote locations on short notice.

Analysis and Reporting

Shorter timelines and less planning are possible when the goals for the project are limited, thereby requiring less complex analysis. Trying to answer many questions from your data increases the complexity and, therefore the length, of analysis.

The quickest forms of analysis rely primarily on field notes or debriefing sessions after each group. For more complex analyses, the major timeline issue is whether the analysis can be accomplished simply by listening to the tapes, rather than waiting for typed transcriptions of them.

The form of the report also has a considerable impact on timelines. An oral presentation with a few bulleted points in an executive summary will shorten the report writing phase. More time is required for full, written reports, starting with brief executive summaries and moving up to detailed written products that may require multiple revisions. Another reporting option that takes additional time is the production of videotapes. Projects that that include a video as part of the report often require an edited "highlights" tape that brings together responses from different sessions, and this will take time to produce.

Add Extra Time If . . .

One of the most difficult challenges is to correctly estimate the time needed for a focus group study. After you make the estimate, you are expected to live with it, unless something unusual happens. Beginning researchers often have an especially difficult time devising accurate time estimates. Recently, a group of veteran focus group researchers offered the following advice:

- *Add 35% more time overall if you're proposing to do something that you've never done before.*
- *Add 20% more time for each stage where a committee has to give approval.*
- *Add 20% more time to the analysis if it includes a formal set of recommendations.*

Considering all of these factors together, it is easy to understand why some focus group projects take only a week or two while others require many months. There is no simple cookie-cutter approach to determining the timeline for a set of focus groups. This is what planning is all about. The basic lesson is that it takes time to work through the factors that can shorten or lengthen a project, but investing this time in planning will lead to a realistic timeline.

4

Personnel and Budgeting

Overview

Planning
Recruiting
Moderating
Analysis and Reporting
Personnel and Budgeting for Smaller Projects
Personnel and Budgeting for Larger Projects
Factors That Affect Personnel and Budgeting Decisions

This chapter outlines the essentials of personnel and budgeting for each of the four basic steps in a focus group project: planning, recruiting, moderating, and analyzing. We consider personnel and budget together, because staff time is almost always the single largest source of expenses.

Just as the planning and timelines in the previous chapter varied between smaller and larger projects, so too will the personnel and budgets. We thus present separate scenarios for smaller and larger projects. We conclude by considering the factors that can increase or decrease a project's personnel and budget requirements.

Planning

The personnel involved in the planning process include, at a minimum, the researcher and the sponsor. When a larger project involves multiple staff members, the planning process will also include input from team members who play major roles in recruitment, moderating, and analysis.

The researcher's first responsibility in the planning process is to determine whether the projected staff and budget are adequate for the expected work. This is especially important when the sponsor is new to focus groups. Sometimes, what appears to be a small, in-house project may actually be larger or more complex. For example, the desired pool of participants may be hard to locate or schedule, or the desired level of detail in the final report may require an extensive analysis. It is thus crucial to identify any problems that will require special staffing or a larger budget as soon as possible. Not dealing with these problems early on may seriously compromise the ultimate quality of the data and the conclusions.

Looking beyond the planning phase itself, the decisions that you make at this point will affect the personnel and budgeting for the project as a whole. Will you use an outside service to do the recruitment? Will you pay the participants? Will you rent a professional facility? Will you serve refreshments or meals? Do you need to prepare "stimulus materials" or other props for use during the group? Will you transcribe audiotapes? And so on. Each of these issues needs to be thought through and decided ahead of time.

Recruiting

This time-consuming task is best accomplished by two or more people who can make calls when participants are most likely to be available to answer them. It is difficult for just one person to accomplish the initial calling in a short time, even if the project entails just two groups and you have a prequalified list from which to recruit. For example, if two groups will each have eight participants and you have to talk to four people in order to schedule someone who is willing and available, this adds up to a total of 64 contacts—and this does not count attempted contacts that are busy, not at home, answered by a machine, and so forth. If you do have multiple people involved in the recruitment effort, it is advisable to have one person who is in charge and supervises the others.

To determine the number of hours involved in recruiting, assume that unsuccessful recruitment contacts will probably take about 5 minutes. A successful contact, however, may require as much as 20 minutes to sign up and schedule a participant, especially if a screening questionnaire or demographic summary is completed. The big unknowns, however, are the number of calls that it will take to make a contact and the number of contacts that it will take to produce a successfully recruited participant. When you are working with a professional recruitment service, it will be able to provide estimates for the costs of all elements of the recruitment, and these will be built into a contract.

Chapter 9 Has More Information on Estimating Recruitment Resources

Participant stipends (also known as incentives, honorariums, or co-op or cooperation fees) are a potential recruitment expense. As discussed in Chapter 9 of this book, one way to make a focus group attractive is to pay cash for participating. Do not assume, however, that you have to pay. If you have a large pool of potential recruits who have intrinsic reasons to participate in a group, then there is often no need to offer a stipend. Instead of cash, participants who are motivated will appreciate good refreshments and a chance for their voices to be heard by an organization that they care about.

When you do pay stipends to participants, they can range from $20 to $50 for members of the general population, and much higher for more specialized samples. In general, the harder you have to look to recruit actual participants for your groups, the more attractive your offer needs to be. Are the desired participants rare or hard to locate? Will they have time available? Are they likely to turn you down without some added incentive?

In addition to personnel costs, recruitment also generates other expenses. Sending confirmation letters to each participant involves printing and postage costs. Telephone recruitment can also generate its own expenses, most notably long distance charges when the participants live outside the local area.

Along with recruiting goes the necessity of locating a place to hold the groups. Chapter 10 describes a range of options for places to hold focus groups, including many that cost nothing. When a neutral location or a nicer room is needed, the lower-cost option is to rent a conference room from a hotel or similar facility. The cost of such rentals varies widely, depending how luxurious the site is, the time blocks that you request, whether you pay for the catering of meals or refreshments, and so forth. As a starting point, assume that it should be possible to find a no-frills room for a single, evening group for $50 to $150. This price will often go down if you either book multiple blocks of time or use the

Chapter 10
Has More on
Choosing
Locations

hotel's catering services; morning rentals may also be cheaper than afternoons or evenings.

The high-cost option is to hire a specialized facility with rooms that are designed for focus groups. A 3-hour block of time for a single group at such a facility is likely to cost $300 to $500; buying a larger block of time for multiple groups may reduce this cost. In some cases, this price compares favorably with the charge for simple meeting rooms in more expensive hotels. Of course, professional facilities offer many other services, although some of these options may come at an added cost, as discussed in Chapter 10.

Professional Facilities: What Do You Get for Your Money?

Professional facilities provide more than just a room in which to hold focus groups. For one thing, these are specialized rooms with a number of useful features, including built-in audiotaping and/or videotaping equipment, as well as a separate viewing area (often behind a one-way mirror) where the sponsor or other observers can monitor the group.

In addition, the staff at the facility typically play a number of roles during the group itself. They will greet and log in participants, serve refreshments to them, act as the moderator's assistant, communicate between the moderator and any observers, and serve as host for any observers in the viewing area. Having someone available to perform these functions at each site allows a solo moderator to travel from location to location during the course of a project and still be assured that efficient procedures will be in place.

Do Not Give Up Control of the Project

One potential cost savings in using professional facilities is that many of them offer "package prices" for a combination of recruitment, room rental, and moderating. In other words, if you hire their recruiters and their moderators along with their room, you get a reduction in the total price. Such package deals are attractive because they offer both savings and convenience. The danger in this approach is that it often means a substantial loss of control over the project. Without hands-on involvement throughout the course of the project, it is difficult to assess the value of the end product. If the results are disappointing, what caused the problem? If the results are exciting, can they truly be believed? You should carefully examine any offer to "do it all for you."

Moderating

A good moderator is key to getting useful data from the focus groups. Two important considerations in making decisions about moderators are their prior experience and their relationships to the participants.

As Volume 4, *Moderating Focus Groups* explains, the factors that point to the choice of an experienced moderator are fairly obvious: Is the project critical to the sponsor? Are the participants difficult or expensive to locate? Will the participants' discussion be challenging either to initiate or control? In each of these cases, it will be wiser to use an experienced moderator rather than risk a poor outcome in the course of "on-the-job training."

The moderator's background and relationship to the participants also affect this personnel decision. The issue here is how the participants will perceive the moderator. Will they think that she or he is indeed open to hearing a wide range of opinions and experiences, or will they perceive this particular moderator as having a hidden agenda? For example, if a moderator is affiliated with the research sponsor, this can lead the participants either to withhold criticism or turn the group into a gripe session.

When a lack of either experience or neutrality means that you cannot use your own staff as moderators, it is necessary to bring in someone from the outside. The major problem with outside moderators is their lack of familiarity with your organization and your goals in this project. Regardless of their background, moderators need to understand the goals of the project. They also need to be comfortable with the discussion guide before moderating the first session. Bringing an outside moderator up to speed may thus require a longer timeline for the planning stage of the project. One strategy for overcoming an outsider moderator's lack of familiarity is to use "dual-moderators," that is, to pair the outsider with a local person who serves as a cofacilitator, as described in *Moderating Focus Groups*.

Fees for professional moderators are similar to consultant fees, and the billing can be done on several different bases. Many moderators bill by the hour in a range from $75 to more than $300 per hour. This kind of expense can be quite reasonable if it is buying the moderator's core expertise at conducting groups. It can also be quite wasteful to pay these kinds of hourly rates for more mundane work such as recruitment. If the moderator or researcher takes responsibility for implementing the entire focus group project (including recruitment, facility rental, and all arrangements), the charge for the project is often based on a per diem, rather than an hourly, amount. The amount that moderators charge per day can range from $750 for a small local project to $1,500 or more for a complex project that is national in scope. Another basis for calculating moderators' fees is on a per-group basis. At the low end, this can cost between $250 and $1,000 per group for straightforward topics where the moderator is not involved in recruitment or analysis. When the moderator has full

Moderating Focus Groups **Has More on When to Use Experienced Moderators**

responsibility for a complex project, the total cost can easily work out to $2,000 to $3,000 per group.

Regardless of the basis for assigning the moderator's fees, be sure you know exactly which expenses are included in the charges. Any contract that you sign with a moderator or outside consultant should specify the costs associated with each of the broad aspects of the work, and who is responsible for which costs.

Using an Outside Moderator May Not Cost Money

What if your need for an outside moderator has more to do with their neutrality rather than their prior experience? Do not assume that using someone from outside your organization means hiring an expensive professional. Although many professional moderators will do some "pro bono" work, it may be easier to exchange moderating services with a partner from your own community. For example, one volunteer organization may "borrow" a moderator from another, or two government agencies may agree to cosponsor a joint training session for their employees and then share the services of these moderators. This is basically a barter arrangement that can go beyond a tit-for-tat exchange of moderating services. For example, one organization might provide a moderator in return for another, different resource that it lacks.

Analyzing and Reporting Focus Group Results Describes the Assistant's Role in Analysis

In addition to a moderator, it is useful to have an assistant to help greet participants as they arrive, serve refreshments, and take care of any emergencies that come up while the group is in progress. Often, the assistant will also observe or make notes on the group process, as discussed in Volume 6, *Analyzing and Reporting Focus Group Results*. In some cases, the assistant may also act as a liaison with any observers who may be watching from behind a one-way mirror or via video. Such assistants may come from your own staff, or, when hiring a professional moderator, they may be included in the basic fees.

Analysis and Reporting

The person who does the moderating also usually does the analysis and reporting. If, however, the moderator's role is limited to conducting the groups, then a researcher who is familiar with the larger project should be in charge of the analysis. Either way, questions about who will do the analysis and prepare the final report need to be answered during the initial planning process.

The amount of staffing for the analysis will be a function of both the number of groups and the level of detail required in the final report. Projects with a large number of groups or a detailed report will require either more time from a single analyst or a larger analysis team. Both options generate higher costs. For complex projects, it often makes sense to have a more expensive professional oversee the work of one or two well-trained but less expensive assistants. For example, hiring an outside professional often means that this person will have the sole responsibility for moderating the groups and writing the report, but he or she may well have assistance in conducting the analysis. It is another matter, however, when the researcher hires a third party or ghostwriter to do the analysis.

There is an increasing tendency for focus group consultants to hire third parties to conduct the analysis and write the report. In principle, this saves money because it substitutes a less expensive person for a more expensive one. The drop in the quality of the analysis may not be worth the savings, however.

Third-Party Analysis

These analysts are third parties in the sense that they do not belong to either the sponsoring organization or the team that designed and conducted the groups. Indeed, the process is sometimes referred to as having a ghostwriter prepare the analysis and report.

In this approach, the third-party analyst reviews copies of the tapes or transcripts and uses a prespecified format to generate the report for a fixed price. For example, the analyst might receive $500 per group to listen to tapes and prepare a three-page final report without verbatim quotes, or $750 per group for a five-page report with quotations.

The obvious concern with this approach is that it may be too removed from the original sponsor's goals. For a complex project with multiple goals, this will almost certainly be a problem. For smaller projects where a simple purpose can be addressed easily within the prespecified reporting format, this may be a lesser concern. Still, there is an unavoidable process of translation when the sponsor's goals are communicated to the analyst via an intermediary, thus increasing the distance between the sponsor's original intent and the final report.

From the sponsor's point of view, it is important to ask any outside consultant about the analysis and report-writing process: How will the analysis be conducted? Who will do that work? Will it be contracted out? Will the report be written according to a prespecified format? Consultants themselves have a corresponding obligation to clarify any circumstances in which the analysis and report writing will be done by someone who was not involved in collecting the data. The bottom line is that sponsors cannot make an informed decisions about a proposed strategy for analysis and report writing unless they know who will be doing this work and how it will done.

An additional cost concern at this stage is the possible transcription of audiotapes or editing of videotapes. Transcripts can be produced from either audiotapes or videotapes. The expense associated with transcribing varies with the expertise of the typist.

For a skilled word processor who has prior experience with group interviews, it typically takes 4 to 6 hours of typing time for each hour of group discussion, at a cost of $20 to $30 per hour. As a rough estimate, this suggests that a 90-minute discussion will cost about $100-150 to transcribe.

Analyzing and Reporting Focus Group Results Discusses the Pros and Cons of Videotaping

Careful thought should be given to videotaping, since its benefits in depicting the discussion can be offset by its effects on the quality of the discussion. If a report is to include video, you will need to decide on the quality of the presentation. Quality ranges from professional productions to home video, and costs will vary accordingly. The level of quality desired will influence decisions on costs of equipment, the need for professional help in filming or editing, the location of the meeting room, and other factors.

Personnel and Budgeting For Smaller Projects

Chapter 3 Describes This Example of a Smaller Project

Smaller focus group projects can be conducted by a minimum of one researcher with one or two support staff if the researcher has sufficient experience with focus groups and is able to work at least half-time on the project for several weeks. To review the general issues associated with personnel and budgeting for smaller projects, we will consider the example that we used in the previous chapter for an in-house project to gather feedback from the users of a service, program, or product. That project called for conducting four groups and took 6 weeks from start to finish. Some of the fundamental assumptions about personnel and budgeting for the project are that:

- A staff member has prior experience with focus group research.
- This person can spend most of her or his time on the project.
- Additional staff members can do the recruiting and assist with other tasks.
- Existing information makes it relatively easy to locate and recruit participants.
- There are no travel costs.
- There will be a brief oral report with a two-page executive summary.

The following budget for this project shows two different categories of costs. In the first column are the actual cash expenditures that are necessary to do the work. In the second column are estimates of the "in-kind" costs associated with using in-house staff to do much of the work.

Although the amounts in the second column do not correspond to actual, out-of-pocket expenses, they are nonetheless important planning considerations. In particular, committing staff to work on this project means that they will not be available for other work. Can the requested staff members really be released from their current assignments, or are there other tasks coming up within the projected time frame that will conflict with this project? In addition, there is at least one circumstance when you would definitely want to include these in-kind costs in your formal budget: when you are writing a grant. Many funding agencies require that grant applications include in-kind and matching contributions, and this use of staff is a major contribution from your organization to the project as a whole.

Budget for a Smaller Project		
	Cash Expenditures	In-Kind Costs
Staffing		
Project manager	—	$2,500
Assistant(s)	—	$1,200
Groups	—	—
Room rental	—	$400
Incentives	$640	—
Refreshments	$240	—
Equipment and supplies		
Telephone	—	$50
Mailing	$32	—
Printing and copying	$40	—
Miscellaneous	$40	—
TOTAL	$992	$4,150

EXAMPLE

Budget for a Smaller Project

The point of this itemized sample budget is to provide a listing of the specific costs that you need to consider. For most projects, you will not need to have a budget with this level of detail. Indeed, it is usually more practical to work with broader budget categories that you can treat flexibly if you need to reallocate resources.

The largest cost is associated with the project manager, who will have primary responsibility for planning, conducting, and analyzing the focus groups. The budget is based on an assumption that this person will devote at least a quarter of his or her time to this project. Although the actual amount of time that the project manager spends on this work will vary from day to day, the breadth of this manager's responsibilities will distinctly limit his or her availability for other assignments.

The actual dollar amount assigned to the project manager comes from an assumed salary of $50,000 per year. This salary level reflects the fact that this person has managerial responsibilities, plus the assumption that she or he is skilled enough to have prior expertise with focus groups. Obviously, a less senior person would have a correspondingly lower salary, but it might also be necessary to adjust the assumption that this person could do the work on a half-time commitment. In particular, if the project manager has relatively little experience with focus groups, it would be wiser to make this project the sole focus of his or her attention.

The budget also assumes two assistants who have primary responsibility for the actual recruitment contacts. Based on the timeline in Chapter 3, the budget assumes that these two clerical assistants will each be working half-time on recruitment for a 2-week period. One of the two will also assist with the groups and be available for clerical tasks during the analysis and report writing phases. The actual budget amount is based on two employees at the $20,000 level each of whom works half time on the project, one for 2 weeks and the other for 4 weeks.

Among the expenses for conducting the groups themselves, the room rental is assumed to be an in-kind donation, based on using either the organization's own space or community facilities. There is, however, an actual cash outlay for incentives to participants. The $640 total is based on a payment of $20 to each of 32 participants (four groups of eight people). Although our assumptions for this project do include the use of an available list of clients or customers, we have included a relatively small cash incentive as a way to ensure the success of the recruitment within the allotted 2-week time frame. Considering that the participants may well have child-care and parking costs, this incentive is probably more a reimbursement than an actual payment. We also include refreshments costs of $7.50 per participant, on the assumption that these groups will be held in the late afternoon and early evening; offering the equivalent of a dinner will help some potential participants fit the group into their schedules. This cost will cover a box lunch and soft drinks.

In the Equipment and Supplies category, the in-kind telephone expense reflects the reality that these machines will not be available for other purposes during the recruitment activities. Mailing expenses of $1 per participant provide for sending confirmation letters to each scheduled person. Printing and copying expenses of $10 per group cover the production of the interview guide, any materials that will be distributed to participants, and the preparation of the executive summary. The final, miscellaneous category includes another estimate of $10 per group for items such as the audiotape that will be recorded in each group, as well as computer disks and other supplies that are necessary throughout the project.

Examining the total costs, the out-of-pocket expenses for this project would be very close to $1,000. Factoring in the staff time involved, the total cost is closer to $5,000. Could you actually get an outside firm to do this work for $5,000? Possibly, if the consultant you were hiring considered this an "easy project" due to prior familiarity with both the topic of the research and the category of participants. Without that background, a consultant would have to build in more time for planning and analysis than we have assumed for this in-house effort.

There are at least four other categories of costs that we have not included in this sample budget:

1. *Benefits and other personnel expenses*

2. *Indirect costs and overheads*

3. *Managerial time*

4. *Inexperience*

Hidden Costs

With regard to benefits, all of our calculations were strictly limited to salary. The actual costs of employees, however, include not just salary but benefits and other personnel expenses (social security, unemployment insurance, workman's compensation, etc.). We have not attempted to show amounts for these items because they vary so widely across organizations. In every case, a more realistic assessment of staff costs would include these expenses. In some cases, "other personnel expenses" may be a required element in your budget, such as in grant applications, or when you are hiring university-based researchers.

Overhead or indirect expenses include all of the facilities and services that are necessary for the most basic aspects of the work. For example, using your own staff means that part of your organization's Accounting and Human Relations operations have been used in support of the project. Similarly, making office space available involves rent, heat, light, janitorial services, and so on. Although these considerations would probably be negligible for a true in-house project, there might well be a line-item expense for "indirect costs" in a formal grant application.

We have also omitted any attempt to estimate the fraction of time that upper-level management would devote to this project. This involvement would be most apparent during the initial planning and final reporting stages.

A final source of hidden costs is inexperience. If this is the first time that your research team is doing focus groups, or if your procedures for these groups are a substantial departure from your past experience, then this can have budgetary consequences. A simple suggestion would be to increase the budget by a "contingency" of 10% to cover unanticipated expenses.

Chapter 3 Describes This Example of a Larger Project

Personnel and Budgeting for Larger Projects

To consider the resources that are necessary for a larger project, we once again flesh out the requirements for the project that we outlined in the previous chapter. This project involved comparing groups of users and nonusers for a service, program, or product at multiple locations. The assumptions for that larger project included:

- A total of eight groups: users and nonusers in each of four regions
- An outside firm to do the recruitment
- A professional consultant to do the moderating and analysis
- A detailed written report

EXAMPLE

Budget for a Larger Project

Budget for a Larger Project

	Costs
Staffing	
Moderator (24 days @ $1,000 a day)	$24,000
Support staff (5 days @ $250 a day)	2,500
Recruitment (80 participants @ $50 each)	4,000
Travel	
Airfare (4 trips @ $1,250 each)	$5,000
Meals and lodging (8 days @ $200 a day)	1,600
Groups	
Facility rental (8 groups @ $300 each)	$2,400
Supplies and equipment (8 groups @ $50 each)	400
Incentives (80 participants @ $40 each)	3,200
Transcription (8 groups @ $150 each)	1,200
TOTAL	$44,300

For this budget, we have not shown any in-kind expenses based on using your own staff. At a minimum, however, there will need to be designated liaisons between the sponsoring organization and the outside consultants. Deciding which people will provide this contact and how much time they will devote to it is an important planning concern, even if it does not show up as a line item in the budget.

The largest expense in the budget, making up nearly half of the total, is the outside consultant. The total of 24 days work is based on the following allocation across the project: 4 days for planning activities, 12 days for moderating groups (including travel time), and 8 days for doing the analysis and report writing. The figure of $1,000 per day is a ballpark estimate; depending upon the topic or the type of participants, the actual figure could be anywhere from half this amount to more than double. The equipment and supply charges include the cost of taping and of any materials that are used in the groups, which are minimal in this case.

During the planning phase, the consultant meets with the sponsor to determine the research design and generate the interview guide. In addition, the consultant takes on the responsibility for selecting the recruitment service and facilities at each location, as well as for making travel arrangements. For a project this size, this will typically require at least three face-to-face meetings: one meeting to lay out the goals and discuss the desired content for the interview; a second meeting to revise the researcher's proposed draft of the interview guide and review the proposed recruitment strategy; and a third meeting to finalize the interview guide and approve the other arrangements.

An outside firm will handle the recruitment phase of this project; because this project uses multiple locations, several firms may be involved, one at each site. The consultant will typically subcontract with these firms to provide the desired number of participants who meet the eligibility requirements for each group. In this case, we have assumed that that the firm will recruit ten participants for each group in order to ensure a desired group size of eight. The charge of $50 per participant is based on an assumption that these participants will be relatively easy to locate through an existing list or data base.

Chapter 9 Discusses How Recruitment Firms Estimate Costs

We have also assumed that the consultant will rent focus group facilities through the same firms that do the recruitment in each location. This produces a somewhat reduced estimate for the cost of renting each facility for two groups, since the room is being supplied as part of a package. This package price also includes refreshments for the participants and an assistant to work with the moderator at each site. Working with professional providers for the recruitment and facilities means that the consultant does not need any other staff during the data collection phase, since the providers will supply any necessary assistance.

We have assumed that this phase will involves 2 full days of work per site. This includes not only moderating a pair of groups at each location but also travel between the sites and confirmation of local arrangements upon arrival. Note that this would be an exceedingly hectic schedule if these sessions were done back-to-back, so the original timeline allows a total of 3 weeks for this work. During this period, the moderator also gives a preliminary oral report to the sponsor.

Rather than an "assistant," we have included a more general charge for support staff. Depending on the moderator that you hire, these people may be more involved with planning or analysis. Either way, it is unlikely that the moderator will work completely without support.

The total budget is close to $45,000. Of course this figure is unlikely to describe any given real project, even if that project might involve eight groups spread across four locations. As already noted, the consultant costs will vary depending on how much expertise is available, and the travel figures here are ballpark estimates at best. Still, this example provides a realistic sense of the cost considerations involved in a project of this size. As with the smaller project, however, there may be hidden costs, and if your research team lacks experience, you would be wise to increase the budget by about 10% to allow for unanticipated costs.

BACKGROUND

Budgeting for Contracts

The total budget is often specified in a contract. For example, a government agency may announce a maximum amount that it is willing to pay to conduct a given number of groups done with a specific set of participants with a completed report by a particular due date. What factors should you consider if you are either offering such a contract or bidding on one?

The least flexible aspects of budgeting are recruitment costs and moderating fees, since they are determined by market forces. The costs for recruitment will be a direct function of who the participants are. Any consultant considering a bid on a contract will have to estimate what it will cost to recruit these participants and subtract that amount from the total budget as an unavoidable up-front cost.

Moderator costs will also be fixed within a relatively narrow band for any given project. Good moderators are always in demand and have no difficulty getting their going rate. If the topic is complex or requires expert knowledge, then the rate will be higher.

This leaves planning and analysis as the two areas where bidders have the most flexibility in responding to contracts. This can be a definite problem when a contract sets a low asking price, since the most obvious way to trim the budget is to cut back on the planning and analysis. For planning, this means offering a standardized set of procedures with little regard to the specifics of the given project. For analysis, cost cutting means spending less time on interpreting and summarizing the data.

In other words, a sponsor who tries to cut back on the cost of a contract for focus groups runs a distinct risk of getting low-quality work due to insufficient planning and analysis.

Factors That Affect Personnel and Budgeting Decisions

Planning

Complex projects will demand either more time or more expertise during the planning process. This translates into higher costs, due to the need for either greater time commitments or more experienced staff. Two common sources of complexity are projects that either use groups in different geographical areas or draw from multiple target populations. In these situations, your planning has to accommodate the issues that may occur in different locations or in different target segments.

Different complexities occur whenever you are working with a target population that is new to you or that presents unusual issues. In this case, you may need the expertise of consultants who know these target populations. Their advice can help you recognize any special characteristics that would affect the recruitment, moderating, or scheduling of the sessions. Some of these characteristics might be cultural norms related to group discussion, appropriate ways to address a person over the telephone, and even appropriate times or locations for holding the sessions.

The planning process is also where you first confront the trade-offs involved in recruiting enough of the right kind of participants. Cash incentives for participants may add to the cost of the project, but offering them may reduce the length of time you need to recruit enough participants. Or, are you willing to accept a set of participants who are less expensive to recruit, even if they are not the ideal target population for your groups?

Food is another planning concern, whether it is either a drawing card in its own right or part of the convenience of scheduling groups near meal times. For some very hard to reach target populations, such as physicians, lawyers, or CEOs, a more elegant catered meal may be a more appropriate incentive than cash. If you are holding a session at the dinner hour, you must provide food for participants. For even the simplest focus group projects, snacks and coffee, juice, or soft drinks before the session help people get comfortable. You need to make these decisions early on, so that you can inform participants what will and will not be available when you schedule them for a session.

Chapter 10 Has
More Information
on Choosing
Locations

Scheduling sessions also means that your initial planning has to include the decision about where to hold the groups. One way to save the cost of renting a state-of-the-art focus group facility is to hold the sessions in a simpler setting. Sometimes, community centers, churches, or local colleges have rooms available for small public meetings for a reasonable fee or donation. If you do use a community setting, be sure that it is conducive to small group discussion and that it is accessible to participants with disabilities.

Recruiting

In recruiting, the single greatest savings of time, and thus money, comes from being able to rely on a preexisting list of qualified participants. The most common alternative is screening the general population to find eligible participants. Screening the general population is more expensive because it takes more time to find enough appropriate participants for the group. If you are considering the use of an existing list, however, be sure that you do not compromise the quality of your data. Sometimes you have a list that does not exactly match your target participants. This creates a trade-off between using a less than ideal set of participants who are easy to recruit versus using more carefully selected participants who require more recruitment effort. In that case, ask yourself which matters more for your particular project: time and expense constraints, or data quality?

Allocating more personnel and budget to recruitment makes sense when you are conducting groups in different geographical locations or outside your local area. Public and nonprofit groups that are trying to minimize costs might do out-of-town recruitment through sister organizations. If you are working with professional recruitment firms, there are times when you may need to hire a different recruitment firm in each location where you are operating, especially if you are also renting professional focus group rooms from these same vendors. Other times, it will be more convenient or cost-effective either to do your own multi-site recruitment or hire a single local firm. Regardless of the options you choose, be sure to allow for the extra work associated with recruiting from multiple locations.

A final cost consideration in recruitment is whether or not you wish to "over-recruit," that is, invite more participants than you really need in order to allow for no-shows. This obviously affects the number of people that you need to recruit. From the present perspective, whether or not you wish to over-recruit is a planning issue. We will argue in Chapter 9 that over-recruitment should be kept to a minimum, but there are circumstances when it may be more advisable. In particular, if you are working with a new category of participants that you have not tried to recruit before, it may be better to over-recruit so that you will be safe rather than sorry. Similarly, if your recruitment staff lacks experience at this task, you may want to have them locate a few extra participants for each session, rather than assume that your unskilled recruiters have successfully convinced everyone to attend.

Chapter 9
Discusses
Over-Recruiting

Moderating

Whether to use your own staff or hire an outside moderator is often the single most expensive consideration in a focus group project. Once again, the trade-off is cost versus the quality of the data.

A third option is to invest in training your own staff so that they acquire expertise in moderating. The cost of sending one staff member to a reputable 2-day training program is typically comparable to what an outside consultant would charge to moderate two to three focus groups. If such training programs are available, that may be a sensible compromise between relying on a novice versus hiring a professional.

Another personnel consideration arises when you need to use more than one moderator, such as when you plan to conduct groups in different geographical locations. You may also want to use more than one moderator if you are conducting a number of local groups within a short time frame. Using multiple moderators often increases the cost of a project, but being able to conduct groups simultaneously may shorten the project timeline enough to justify the expense. If you do use multiple moderators, be sure that they all understand the goals of your project, have discussed the guide with the researcher, and have reasonably similar styles for moderating focus groups.

Whenever a project includes groups outside your local area, you also need to consider travel costs. One option is to hire a single moderator who will travel to the remote sites. At a minimum, this requires you to factor in the moderator's transportation, food, and lodging costs. In addition, many outside consultants charge their full rate for days they are traveling, since this may deprive them of a day's work. The alternative option of hiring moderators who live at the remote site saves the travel expenses but raises questions about how well they understand the project and whether the group will be truly comparable. In some cases, it may make sense to bring all of the moderators together for a training session, but this can cost just as much as moving a single moderator from place to place. A cheaper alternative is to accomplish this training through a telephone or video conference.

Analysis and Reporting

Generally, the project's primary researcher does the analysis and report writing. When this researcher is someone other than the moderator, there needs to be input from those who attended the groups. This input may come not only from the moderator but also from other observers. These observers often include representatives from the project sponsor, who discuss their reactions with the research team following the group.

Another way to involve the sponsor in the analysis process is through preliminary reporting (see the example of the larger project in this chapter and the previous one). A preliminary report allows the researcher to talk to the sponsor about the meaning of the data and the conclusions and recommendations that can be drawn from them. Clarifying these issues in advance can both shorten the time it takes the researcher to produce a report and increase the value of that report to the sponsor.

If the analysis uses either videotapes or transcripts, additional personnel and budgeting decisions must be made. If you are going to transcribe tapes of the discussions, the major issue is whether you pay for an outside service or use your own staff and equipment to do this in-house. If you will be videotaping, note that professional focus group facilities charge an extra fee for this service.

**Doing
Transcriptions
In-House**

There are two basic considerations in having available staff do transcriptions: experience and equipment. If there is no one who has prior experience transcribing focus groups, someone who types individual dictation may work out. Recognize, however, that group interviews do present another level of challenge. Even excellent dictation typists may not be equally quick or accurate in transcribing the give-and-take of a group discussion. It is thus unwise to try to save money by doing transcriptions in-house unless you are certain that someone has the necessary skills.

With regard to equipment, it definitely helps to have a transcription tape deck with a pedal control. This allows typists to pause and/or rewind the tape without removing their fingers from the keyboard while capturing difficult passages. Regardless of the type of tape deck, a good pair of earphones will be appreciated by both the typist and others in the same office.

When you have transcription equipment but lack experienced typists, another option is to use a temporary service. Many of them can supply experienced focus group typists who will do the work at your site for a price below what it would cost to hire an outside transcription typist.

Overall, from planning through analysis, personnel and budgeting issues pose a series of trade-offs. Some options cost less, while others either produce higher quality data or get things done more quickly. Different projects will have different priorities, and you will need to make your decisions accordingly.

5

Deciding on the Degree of Structure

Overview

Knowing Your Goals Is Crucial
More Structure Emphasizes the Research Team's Focus
Less Structure Emphasizes the Group's Interests
Structure Includes Both Question Content
and Moderator Style
Moderately Structured Groups

Just how focused should a focus group be? Do you want the discussion to center on topics that you provide, or do you want the participants to pursue their own directions? Or, do you want to strike a balance between your agenda and the participants' insights?

Depending on how you write the questions in the interview guide and how the moderator leads the group, your project can consist of either more structured groups, where the research team's interests predominate, or less structured groups, where the participants' interests have priority.

Because the degree of structure determines the kind of data that the discussions produce, it will influence every aspect of the project. It will influence how the questions are written, how the moderator interacts with the participants, and how the analysis is done. Hence, Chapters 5 through 8, which deal with decision making, begin with the fundamental question of how structured the discussions will be.

Knowing Your Goals Is Crucial

Chapter 2 Discusses the Importance of Goals

Chapter 2 of this volume emphasized the importance of goals, and this is especially true for decisions about the degree of structure. How you conduct the group depends on the kind of information you want.

Some projects begin with a very distinct set of questions, and the groups provide the answers. If the project goal is to answer predetermined questions, this calls for a more structured approach that keeps the discussion focused on the issues that need to be addressed. The interview guide or question route in a more structured project will thus define a set of topics and provide clear directions about the amount of time to devote to each of them. The moderator's goal in a more structured project is to keep each group on task. Together, the guide and the style of moderating in a more structured project create a discussion that emphasizes the research team's interests and concerns.

EXAMPLE

A Project With a Relatively High Degree of Structure

Why do some patients with Alzheimer's disease get diagnosed when their symptoms are very mild, while other patients do not receive the diagnosis until their memory problems are quite advanced? Are some families simply having trouble recognizing the early stages of memory problems? Or are there other, more complicated issues that keep families from acting on the symptoms of this very troubling and debilitating disease?

When we investigated this issue, we chose a set of structured groups that sought to explain the difference between families that sought diagnosis when symptoms of Alzheimers were still quite mild versus those who did not seek diagnosis until the symptoms were more advanced.

By asking the same questions in one set of groups where caregivers had acted when the symptoms were either less severe and another set of groups where caregivers had acted when the symptoms were more advanced, we could compare the factors that differentiated these families. In addition, by organizing our questions around the history of each case (e.g., "What were the first symptoms that you each can remember?"), we obtained a consistent account of each family's experiences.

The participants were quite willing not only to share their own stories but also to hear others' stories. This made it easy to collect the history of each case in an orderly fashion, beginning with questions about the earliest stages of the disease and then proceeding to questions about later changes, first contacts with doctors, all who were involved in making decisions, when the diagnosis actually occurred, and so on. The moderator's job was to make sure that each person told the relevant part of his or her family's story in response to each question.

By comparing the groups that acted on milder versus more severe symptoms, we learned that this difference was due more to how families reacted to symptoms rather than whether they recognized the symptoms. In particular, we learned that the reaction to symptoms was tightly connected to the implications that this illness had for the family, since the progressive loss of independence that goes with Alzheimer's disease meant that the patient was going to need a caregiver. Deciding to seek a diagnosis was thus often a decision about caregiving, and that decision could be quite complex and stressful.

A different kind of project starts by not even knowing what the right questions are; focus groups reveal what needs to be known. If the goal is exploratory, this calls for a less structured approach that can discover the range of issues that need to be understood. The interview guide in a less structured project will typically include open-ended questions that spark the group's curiosity about the overall topic. The moderator's goal in a less structured project is to help the group explore the topic in a way that generates new insights. Together, the guide and the style of moderating in a less structured project create a discussion that emphasizes the participants' interests and concerns.

What happens to family caregivers when those for whom they are caring must move to a nursing home? How do the caregivers' lives change? Does their stress level truly drop, or do they just move from one set of problems to another?

When we investigated these questions, we chose an exploratory approach that used less structured focus groups because, at that time, very little was known about family caregivers of people in nursing homes.

In keeping with our unstructured approach, we asked just one basic question: When you think about your caregiving, what kinds of things make your life easier and what kinds of things make it harder?

In every group, this one broad question proved sufficient to generate a prolonged and lively discussion. The fact that the participants easily became highly involved in the discussion meant that we could also use a less structured approach to moderating. In most cases, our moderators did not even sit at the same table as the participants! Instead, they sat nearby and monitored two things: Was the conversation becoming stressful for the participants, and was the discussion covering both the things that made their lives easier and harder?

EXAMPLE

A Project With a Very Low Degree of Structure

By hearing caregivers' own accounts of their experiences with nursing homes, we learned about the unique challenges that they faced. In particular, caregivers in nursing homes often went from being in charge of every aspect of their family member's care to playing a relatively minor role in a formally organized health-care facility. Yet they, rather than the staff, were the ones who knew the patient best and cared about her or him the most. We learned that this combination of caring about the person but not providing the care could be a source of tremendous stress.

More Structure Emphasizes the Research Team's Focus

The basic purpose for more structured groups is to produce answers to the research team's questions. For this approach, both the interview guide and the moderator emphasize learning as much as possible about a predetermined set of topics. The decision to use a more structured approach thus requires that you already know what the right questions are.

The obvious strength of the more structured approach is its ability to deliver a maximum amount of well-targeted information. The downside, however, is an inability to learn about issues that are not included within the narrowly focused set of predetermined issues. What if you only think you know what the right questions are, but in reality you have omitted a crucial issue? A highly structured set of questions would limit your ability to uncover this missing information. And even if the group might try to raise it, a more structured moderating style would redirect the discussion back to the preset topics.

When you know exactly what you want, then the more structured approach is the best choice. Before making this decision, however, it is important to step back and consider whether you truly do know the right questions, since highly structured groups will limit the information that you get.

EXAMPLE

A Decision to Use a More Structured Group

As one of its responsibilities, a new intergovernmental agency was to conduct a survey of local citizens on the "critical issues" facing their community. In this case, the goals of the overall project were quite specific: to conduct a telephone survey where local citizens would rank a list of ten issues in order of importance. The goals for the focus groups were equally specific: to produce this list of ten issues. In particular, the survey required a list that would reflect the major issues in the community and that would state these issues in ways that members of the public could easily understand.

The guide for the interviews divided the discussions into three phases. First, the moderator had each participant write down three issues that he or she thought were important to the local community. Second, the group sorted their various suggestions into coherent categories that the moderator listed on easel sheets. Finally, the participants selected the items in each category that would work best in a survey question.

In each of these three stages, the moderator exercised careful control over the group. First, the moderator worked with the participants to help them generate their initial suggestions in private. Then she worked with the group to construct categories by collecting each list of similar suggestions onto a separate sheet of easel paper. Finally, she had each participant place colorful, self-adhesive "dots" next to the items that they recommended for the survey, creating a visual display of which items were most popular.

After comparing the discussions from four groups, the research team selected the ten categories that appeared most consistently. They also compared the labels that participants had come up with for these categories to generate the wordings for the actual survey questions.

Less Structure Emphasizes the Group's Interests

Less structured groups are most useful for exploratory purposes. Listening to what the participants choose to discuss in a less structured group reveals *their perspective* on the research topic. For this approach, both the interview guide and the moderator emphasize learning as much as possible about what is important to the participants.

The goal in less structured groups is to discover new ideas and insights. The downside of this approach, however, is that the groups can be quite erratic in terms of their productivity. Within any one group, it can be difficult to tell when the discussion is leading up to an exciting insight, or just meandering. This poses a considerable challenge for moderators: Should they let the discussion continue in an apparently unproductive direction, or should they move on at the risk of missing valuable information?

A further difficulty comes up in the analysis of less structured groups. Because the questions are quite broad, and because each group is free to take a question wherever it wishes, it is difficult to make systematic comparisons across groups. This is not a problem when your primary goal is to generate new ideas, so you don't really need to compare which ideas came up in which groups. If, however, you do want to make consistent comparisons about how different groups responded to a set of key topics, then you should probably avoid less structured groups.

Because of their emphasis on discovery and exploration, less structured groups are the best choice when you are uncertain about what you need to know. When you do have clear-cut goals, open-ended discussions in less structured groups are an inefficient way to produce information that directly addresses these goals.

EXAMPLE

A Decision to Use a Less Structured Group

A managed health care plan had just extended its population to cover senior citizens, and the staff now wished to design an exercise program for them. One group of managers wanted to investigate whether these older participants would use the plan's existing exercise programs in gyms and health clubs. The majority of the managers, however, believed that this was too narrow a topic. In particular, if the focus groups showed that seniors did not wish to use the existing exercise programs, then the managers would have few ideas about what alternatives to offer. Consequently, they chose to use a less structured, more exploratory approach.

The guide for these groups consisted of three broad topics. The sessions started with the participants talking about the things that they had enjoyed doing during the past week. Next, the discussions shifted from enjoyable activities to the things that the participants did to "keep themselves active." Finally, the participants talked about ways that they might increase their level of physical activity.

The moderators were to facilitate rather than direct these discussions. At the start, they mostly encouraged participants to tell stories and give concrete examples about the activities they enjoyed doing. In steering the discussion toward "keeping active," the moderators first let the participants interpret being active in their own terms, only gradually moving them toward an emphasis on physical activity. In the final sections, the moderators avoided a narrow discussion of exercise per se, in favor of a more general examination of where physical activity fit into the lives of these seniors.

The results suggested that there were two distinctly different segments of seniors. Some of them wished to increase their level of physical activity by doing things that matched their existing routines, such as gardening and walking pets. But there was also a segment that was very interested in organized exercise programs, so long as the sessions were specifically designed for and limited to people their own age.

Structure Includes Both Question Content and Moderator Style

KEY POINT

Questions, Moderating, and Degree of Structure

In more structured groups, the content of the discussion is controlled by the questions in the interview guide, and the group dynamics are controlled by the moderator. In less structured groups, the participants have more leeway to determine the content of their discussions, and the moderator uses a flexible approach to create a productive group dynamic.

Less Structured Groups

Questions: Typically use a smaller number of broadly focused questions. Questions invite participants to explore the topic, and they are thus open-ended.

Moderating: The moderator typically gives the group the freedom to pursue its own interests. The goal is to learn the participants' perspective on the topic, so the moderator encourages them to share their thoughts, feelings, and experiences.

More Structured Groups

Questions: Typically use a larger number of narrowly focused questions. Questions address the researcher's or sponsor's specific goals, and they are thus direct and to the point.

Moderating: The moderator typically exercises tight control over the group's dynamics. The goal is to keep the group focused on the topic at hand, so the moderator is in control of the discussion.

The Less Structured Approach to Questions

One of the most useful features of the less structured approach to focus groups is that you don't necessarily need to know the interview questions in advance. Try to imagine doing a survey, or even a one-to-one qualitative interview, if you don't know what the questions are! Groups do not have this problem. Once the participants start discussing the topic, they can react to each other. If they are at all interested in the topic, their conversation will very rapidly take on a life of its own. At their best, less structured groups allow the research team the luxury of listening to and learning from the participants.

The goal in less structured groups is to find a few questions that not only interest the participants but also get them to talk about the topics that interest the research team. In other words, less structured groups are *not* unfocused groups. Instead, they are focused on broader topics. This goal of exploring broad topics is matched by a broad, open-ended set of interview questions.

Consider the question from the previous example that used less structured groups to study family caregiving: "What makes your life easier and what makes it harder?" In fact, this question would work well in discussions of many different stressful life events. For the participants, it asks about precisely the experiences that matter most to them. For the researcher, it targets the forms of stress and coping that matter most to the participants.

Very few projects will use an approach that is so unstructured that it consists of only a single question. Less structured approaches where the interview guide contains three to five questions are more common. The first question is often autobiographical, or it may ask about general positive and negative responses to the topic of interest. Such broad opening questions help to get a discussion started, and so they are widely used in all kinds of focus groups. In less structured groups, the responses to this question are an important source of data in themselves, and not just a means to foster a relaxed group dynamic. Consequently, the discussion of a broad opening question will typically last longer in a less structured approach. One third or more of the time in a less structured group may be given over to responses to a broad opening question. Of course, this puts a premium on selecting a good opening question—one that interests both the participants and the research team.

Developing Questions for Focus Groups Describes Options for Opening Questions

The More Structured Approach to Questions

More structured groups are likely to contain more questions in the interview guide. It is possible to ask more questions in a more structured approach both because the questions are narrowly focused and because the moderator ensures that the discussion does not waste time by straying too far from the topic.

Simply having a lot of questions is not, however, an indication that you should use more structure. Too often, a large number of questions is a sign that there is no consensus on what the research is about. Trying to move the discussion through a large number of divergent questions by using a tightly structured approach seldom works. The match between a highly structured approach and a large number of questions is appropriate only when you can write a well-ordered interview guide that flows from one question to the next in a way that captures the participants' interests. Creating this kind of flow in the questions depends, once again, on being clear on the goals of the research. When those goals consist of a coherent set of issues that need to be addressed, there will be little difficulty in producing a logically ordered set of questions that generate a lively discussion.

Avoid Having Too Many Questions

The Less Structured Approach to Moderating

In less structured groups, the moderator does more to facilitate rather than direct the discussion. Because the purpose of such groups is to explore the participants' thinking, the moderator works to create a climate where the participants are willing to share their feelings and experiences.

The instructions that the moderator gives at the beginning of the group can be adjusted to channel the participants' expectations toward a less structured discussion. For example, the moderator could explain his or her role as "listening to all the different things you have to say" and "helping to make sure that we hear from each of you." Notice that these instructions use "you" to address the participants, so they all are aware of the expectation that they will contribute to the discussion.

In addition, the instructions in a less structured group might include a request to hear "a wide range of different points of view." During the discussion, the moderator would reinforce these initial instructions with probes and follow-up questions such as the following:

- *Who else has some thoughts about this—maybe something a little different?*
- *What else have people experienced in this area?*
- *You've been discussing several different ideas; what haven't we heard yet?*
- *Remember, we want to hear all your opinions; who has something else?*

EXAMPLE

Probing in a Less Structured Group

The More Structured Approach to Moderating

Moderators in more structured groups need to be relatively directive to keep the group on topic. Once again, it helps to build this into the participants' expectations during the introduction. For example:

"We have a fairly full agenda today, so I'll apologize in advance if I have to cut off the discussion at any point. I don't want to be impolite, but I may have to interrupt and bring us back to the main topic if we get too far afield. Or I may have to break in and move us along to the next question, so we have enough time to get through all the topics we need to discuss."

EXAMPLE

Instructions in a More Structured Group

Notice that these instructions avoid the word *you* so that no individual participant will feel singled out if the moderator does break into the discussion. Instead, these instructions portray a group goal of getting through a relatively lengthy list of specific topics. These instructions all make it clear, however, that the moderator does have an agenda and that she or he is in control of the group. If it actually becomes necessary to break into the discussion, these instructions provide the justification. For example:

> "Let me just jump in here. . . . (pause) Remember how I said at the beginning that I might have to move the discussion along if we were getting tight on time? Well, now we do need to get on to our next question. That way, we can cover all the questions and still get finished right on time. So, now I'd like you to . . ."

Or,

> "I think I need to come in and do that thing I mentioned in the beginning, to bring us back to the main question, so that we can cover our full agenda . . . (pause). What about (repeat basic question); who can say more about that?"

Moderately Structured Groups

This chapter has emphasized the contrast between more and less structured groups as an aid to making decisions about group structure. Choosing an appropriate degree of structure depends on understanding the differences between more and less structured approaches. Realistically, however, many projects choose a compromise using a moderate degree of structure.

Moderately structured groups are most appropriate when a project calls for learning about both the research team's focus and the participants' interests. Just as with more structured and less structured approaches, the decision to use a moderately structured approach to focus groups requires a deliberate match between the project's goals and that degree of structure. It is not appropriate to choose a moderate degree of structure purely as a compromise because there is no agreement on the project's goals. Nor is it appropriate to think of a moderate degree of structure as a kind of "default value"—something you always use unless there is a compelling reason to do something else. Instead, the best way to select a moderate degree of structure is by consciously rejecting the other alternatives. Are you trying to learn the answers to a set of well-defined questions? Are you trying to learn as much as you can about a relatively unexplored area? If neither of these goals matches your project, then you may well want to consider a moderate degree of structure.

Because moderately structured groups are the most common form of focus groups, most of the material in this kit is directed to conducting such groups. In particular, Volume 3, *Developing Questions for Focus Groups,* provides many substantive suggestions for putting together moderately structured interview guides. Similarly, Volume 4, *Moderating Focus Groups,* provides detailed advice on how to balance the discussion between the researcher's focus and the group's interests.

Developing Questions for Focus Groups **and** *Moderating Focus Groups* **Give Advice About Balancing the Interests of Researchers and Participants**

One specific strategy for implementing a moderate degree of structure is a "funnel design." The analogy is to a discussion that moves from broader to narrower topics. As the volume on Developing Questions for Focus Groups *notes, this movement from general to specific is a frequent aspect of interview guides in focus groups.*

The Top of the Funnel: One or two broad, open-ended questions

The funnel begins with a wide-open question that lets participants express their own thoughts on the research topic. This part of the discussion is less structured. Letting the participants begin by exploring the topic from their own perspective creates the opportunity to discover new insights or uncover unanticipated issues. During this part of the group, moderators usually minimize their own involvement while encouraging all members of the group to participate in the discussion.

BACKGROUND

The Funnel Approach to Moderately Structured Groups

The Middle of the Funnel: Three or four central topics

The central, and usually longest, part of the discussion pursues a set of predetermined, but broadly defined topics. These are things the research team knows that it wants to hear about, and the goal is to hear about them in a wide-ranging and detailed fashion. If these issues are indeed central to the topic, they will undoubtedly arise in response to the opening question, so the transition to a more focused discussion is quite natural. Here, the moderator typically takes a more directive approach so that the group concentrates on the core topics.

The Bottom of the Funnel: Several specific questions

The funnel concludes with sharply focused discussions of narrowly defined issues. Once again, this can be a natural transition, since the previous discussion usually provides a basis for both raising and nailing down these specific concerns. At this point, the moderator is likely to be seeking specific answers to specific questions.

6

Deciding on the Group Composition

Almost every aspect of a focus group project depends on who the participants are. From recruitment to analysis, all your other decisions are contingent upon the composition of the focus groups. The right group composition will generate free-flowing discussions that contain useful data. The wrong group composition may bring together people who have little to say to each other or who may carry on lively conversations that have little relevance to your needs and goals. Decisions about the group composition are thus a crucial aspect of successful planning.

Sampling Strategies for Focus Groups

Focus Groups Rely on Purposive Sampling

Each research method requires choices about who will serve as the sources of the data, and those choices differ from one method to the next. The strategies for selecting samples in focus groups are quite different from those in survey research or experimental designs. Like most other qualitative methods, focus groups rely on *purposive samples*. A purposive sampling strategy chooses the focus group participants according to the project's goals. As the name implies, the selection of the participants follows directly from the purposes of the project.

Consider the following examples and note how, in each case, the purpose of the research determines the choice of who will be in the focus groups.

- A business conducts focus groups with people who are distinctly different from its current customers, in order to target new "market segments."
- A government agency conducts focus groups with clients who are moderately satisfied with their services, in order to hear about both what the agency is doing right and wrong.
- A service agency follows up on a new program by conducting focus groups among those who expressed an interest in the program but never actually enrolled, in order to evaluate its recruitment efforts.

Purposive sampling is very different from the random sampling that is so common in survey samples. The reason for this divergence is the fundamental difference between the goals of focus groups and the goals of surveys. The goal in surveys is to generalize to larger populations by collecting numerically precise data, and this requires selecting a random sample that will cover the entire range of the larger population. The goal in focus groups is to gain insight and understanding by hearing from people in depth, and this requires selecting a purposive sample that will generate the most productive discussions in the focus groups.

Why not use random samples for focus groups, just the way surveys do? One simple answer is that the number of people in most focus group projects is too small to produce an accurate representation of a larger population. Survey samples typically require hundreds or even thousands of people, while a focus group project with 100 participants would be quite large. A more important point, however, is that a random sample of people may not have much to say about your topic. Focus groups work best when they generate lively discussions, and that may not happen in a random collection of participants. So, focus groups composed of random samples can be "the worst of both worlds," since they are unlikely to yield either productive group discussions or useful representations of a larger population.

Random sampling to achieve generalizability in surveys is different from randomly selecting focus group participants from an existing list. In this latter case, the reason for randomizing the choice of participants is to eliminate any bias in the selection process.

One very common strategy for eliminating bias when working with an existing list is to use systematic random sampling. This procedure presumes that you have a relatively long list of potential participants, and then you contact every n-th person. For example, if you had a list of 250 people, you might choose every tenth name on your list. When you reach the end of the list, you wrap back to the beginning, skipping over anyone whom you have already selected. This procedure eliminates any chance that the biases or preferences of the research team will influence who is chosen from the list.

BACKGROUND

Random Sampling Versus Random Selection From a List

Often, researchers want to say they used random samples for their focus groups because it lends an aura of credibility to the research. If the goal is truly to minimize bias, *random selection* may well be justified. But what are the practical implications of randomly selecting your participants from an existing list? In essence, this says two things: (1) you are equally interested in what everyone on the list has to say, and (2) everyone on this list is equally able to talk about your topic. If your list is well suited to your purposes, it may meet both of these criteria; if, however, your list fails either of these tests, then you need to use a more purposive strategy in selecting your participants.

The sampling strategies in surveys and focus groups do share some fundamental features: They both use systematic procedures and well-defined criteria to select the research participants. This contrasts with "convenience samples" and self-selected samples. Convenience samples emphasize the ease of obtaining the participants, as opposed to using well-defined, purposive selection criteria. If groups composed of "just anyone" will truly meet your purposes, then you might use a convenience sample, but this a very rare circumstance.

Self-selected samples are used more often than convenience samples, but they too can present problems. Common examples of self-selected samples include volunteers who respond to notices or advertisements, people who attend public forums or open meetings, and so forth. Because you have not selected them, you really have no idea what larger population they represent. Worse still, the very factors that motivate them to participate may make

Involving Community Members in Focus Groups **Has Exercises on Sample Selection**

them different from other people. For example, these might be people who have volunteered to participate because they like your organization, so they are trying to do you a favor. On the other hand, these might be people with an ax to grind who have sought out your focus groups as one more opportunity to get someone to listen to them. Either way, you will end up with a biased sense of what people have to say.

Bias is the real danger in using either convenience samples or self-selected samples. Whenever the participants in your research differ in some substantial way from the people you want to hear from, you have a problem with bias. By being careful and systematic in selecting your focus group participants, you can minimize bias. Eliminating bias is an important goal in purposive sampling. If you have a purpose for selecting your sample, then you must make sure that you actually reach people who fit this purpose. Although focus group samples will seldom need to be as scientifically representative as survey samples, this is no excuse for using sloppy or biased selection procedures!

Creating a Comfortable, Productive Conversation Is the Key

There are two basic considerations that go into determining the composition of a set of focus groups:

1. the participants' comfort in talking to each other about the topic, and
2. your goals for creating productive discussions about the topic.

It will do you little good to bring together a category of people who interest you if they are not comfortable conversing with one another. Likewise, there is not much point in generating a lively discussion that fails to address your research goals. As a general rule, focus groups work best when what interests the participants also interests you.

From the participants' point of view, the composition of the group will influence whether they can maintain a free-flowing conversation. The emphasis here is on the composition of each separate focus group. Who the participants are in a given group will have a tremendous influence on their group dynamics. You thus need to keep the compatibility of the participants in mind as you determine the composition of each group. These issues will be the subject of the next section, on homogeneity.

From your point of view, the composition of the full set of groups in the project matters as much as the composition of each separate group. Often, this requires varying the composition from group to group. Varying the composition of the groups not only encourages a comfortable group dynamic within each separate group but also creates the opportunity for useful comparisons across the full set of groups. If you suspect that different types of participants will have different perspectives on the topic, then sorting them into separate groups will maximize both their compatibility within groups and your ability to make comparisons between groups. These issues will be the subject of a later section on segmentation.

Both of these basic considerations point to creating homogeneity within each separate group, while allowing for considerable diversity across the full set of groups. This general strategy is called "segmentation."

KEY POINT

Homogeneous Groups Can Meet Both Your Needs and Those of Participants

Homogeneity: The Need for Compatible Participants

In determining the composition of individual focus groups, compatibility is the key concern. When the participants perceive each other as fundamentally similar, they can spend less time explaining themselves to each other and more time discussing the issues at hand. In contrast, mixed groups may spend a good deal of time getting to know each other and building trust before they feel safe enough to share personal information—if they ever reach this level of comfort.

Note that asking whether the participants are compatible can be very different from asking whether they have the experiences and beliefs that you want to hear about. Bringing together people who interest you is a necessary first step, but it is not sufficient. Generating a productive discussion requires a good group dynamic, and that depends on the compatibility of the participants.

EXAMPLE

An Unwise Decision to Use Mixed Groups

A major national consulting firm was trying to expand into a new industry where it had never operated before. For its first project, it worked with a large firm that had a long history of conflict between its field staff, who were in charge of the day-to-day productivity of the organization, and its headquarters staff, who were in charge of the administrative functions.

The consulting firm brought together focus groups that mixed field staff and headquarters staff to discuss these problems. Unfortunately, these groups all showed a consistent pattern of poor group dynamics. On the one hand, the field staff participants became visibly alienated, contributing less and less to the discussion as the group proceeded. On the other hand, the headquarters staff took over the discussion, contributing detailed examples of all the ways that the field staff made their work harder. As a result, the focus groups degenerated into a "gripe session" for the headquarters staff, producing almost no data about the field staff's perspective on the problem.

To understand what went wrong, the consultants conducted a few one-to-one interviews with the overly silent members of the field staff. What they learned was that the field staff were explosively angry about what had happened in the focus groups. In reality, they had as many complaints about the headquarters staff as vice versa, but they did not feel safe voicing them in a mixed group. The reason was that the field staff felt they were at the mercy of the headquarters staff, who controlled the processing of all their paperwork. Furthermore, many members of the field staff believed that the headquarters staff used this power in a petty and vindictive fashion. One example came from a field staffer who had tried to suggest a way to improve the processing of travel reimbursement requests. The headquarters staff not only refused to consider any changes in their procedures but also retaliated by repeatedly delaying that field staffer's reimbursement requests, forcing him to bear the expenses out of pocket.

If the original focus groups had been divided into two homogeneous segments, the concerns of both sides would have been heard. Instead, the mixed groups produced unbalanced data. Worse still, they added to the ongoing animosity that the consultants were hired to correct!

The classic way to achieve compatibility is by bringing together groups of homogeneous participants. Background or demographic characteristics are one common basis for selecting homogeneous focus groups. The most common demographic characteristics for determining group composition are the following:

- Gender
- Race or ethnicity
- Age
- Location or residence
- Education level
- Occupation
- Income
- Marital status or family composition

It is important to understand that homogeneity on demographic characteristics is a means to increase compatibility, not an end in itself. Similarity on outward criteria will only take you so far. In many cases, the participants' experiences matter more than their demographics. For example, mixing together those who choose to use a product or service with those who do not will often produce a tense group dynamic, no matter how demographically homogeneous the participants are. Similarities on key experiences can also override demographic differences, as I have learned in groups where participants who were seemingly very different had each experienced the same stressful life event, such as widowhood or caring for a family member with Alzheimer's disease.

KEY POINT

Compatibility on Shared Experiences Often Matters More Than Demographic Characteristics

Some marketing researchers claim that men and women have such different group dynamics that it is often advisable to separate them. This may well be true for certain categories of consumer products, but social scientists and researchers in organizational settings have found fewer difficulties in conducting mixed-sex groups.

What is crucial here is whether there are gender differences in how people experience or respond to the specific topic of the research. For example, coworkers discussing company procedures for doing the routine aspects of their jobs are unlikely to have gendered differences that will affect their group dynamics. If, however, the topic were issues in combining work and family or perceptions of factors that affect promotions, then there might well be good reasons for conducting separate groups of men and women.

CAUTION

Mixing Groups by Gender

Whether any given demographic characteristic will affect the compatibility of the participants depends on the topic of the research. For example, I once conducted a group about retirement plans that required all the participants to come from the same age group and to work at similar jobs; however, the group was thoroughly mixed with regard to gender and race. Everything went well until it became apparent that some of the participants had considerably more savings than others. Those who felt that they had no choice but to continue working expressed a thinly veiled resentment toward those who were looking forward to a comfortable retirement. Although we had created homogeneity with regard to income by selecting participants with similar jobs, we had failed to recognize the importance of differences in assets and investments. Sometimes, there is simply no way to know what the key elements of compatibility are until you have done a group or two.

When you are unsure about whether the potential participants in a focus group will be truly compatible, it may be necessary to start with the more limited goal of avoiding conflict. The sharing of ideas and experiences is at the heart of focus groups, and this requires a climate of mutual respect. At a minimum, the composition of each focus group should minimize suspicion and open disagreement.

**Authority
Relationships
Are a Problem**

*The Focus Group
Guidebook
Discusses
Ethical Issues*

In work settings, it is almost always unwise to mix together workers and those who supervise them. Even if those in authority insist that the workers under them are free to say anything they wish, people will seldom speak freely in front of those with the power to reward and punish them.

Authority relationships can raise ethical concerns as well, as described in The Focus Group Guidebook. *Even when supervisors are not in the group, they can have an equally chilling effect on the discussion if they are watching from behind a mirror. Similar concerns arise when supervisors will have access to tapes and transcripts. In any of these circumstances, it is important to know up front who will have access to the data and to inform the participants accordingly.*

Issues involving authority relationships also arise outside the workplace. Mixing government officials with their clients or church leaders with their congregations is almost certain to create tension. Some ethnic groups may also hesitate to speak openly to elders or members of leading families. Here and throughout, the central concern is the participants' sense of comfort and safety.

Compatibility problems can also arise when different categories of participants have different ways of expressing themselves. To have a successful group discussion, the participants need to share information with each other. Although difficulties in group dynamics are most obvious when different categories of participants have very different perspectives on the topic, issues of communication style can also create incompatibilities. Thus, if two different types of participants have very different ways of talking about the same content, this would point toward separating the participants into more homogeneous groups.

EXAMPLE

**Different Ways
of Expressing
Similar
Experiences**

A research team was using focus groups to develop a media campaign that would promote exercise. Because the existing literature indicated that men and women had different approaches to exercise, they had already decided to conduct separate groups by gender. There was, however, little prior guidance about whether or not European Americans and African Americans had compatible views on exercise.

To be on the safe side, the research team decided to conduct separate groups by race. In retrospect, they felt that it would have been possible to combine the women's groups across racial lines but that the men's groups were quite different for blacks and whites. In particular, what was different was not so much their attitudes toward exercise but their ways of expressing these attitudes. The white males tended toward an earnest expression of the value of exercise, while their black counterparts were much more vocal and excited. Although the content of what they were saying was very similar, it would have been hard to create a free-flowing discussion between the two sets of participants.

In projects such as this, where the goal is to design media messages, learning of differences in communication style can prove to be very valuable.

Although concerns about compatibility typically lead to a homogeneous composition for individual focus groups, there certainly are situations when a purposive sampling strategy will point toward bringing together a more heterogeneous set of participants. One obvious case is when the goals of the project require information about interaction between different categories of participants. For example, an interest in either cross-cultural communication or intergroup decision making could lead to the decision to use a mixed group. In other cases, the group dynamics of mixed groups may be an advantage rather than a disadvantage. In particular, when participants do have different perspectives on a topic, it makes sense to ask them to take time to describe and explain their experiences and ideas. This gives the researchers an opportunity to uncover and explore assumptions that would otherwise be taken for granted among peers.

A research team was investigating how to get more low-income women to sign up for a government benefit program. Their original plan was to conduct separate groups among users and nonusers of this program, however, they were initially dismayed to discover that some of the women they had recruited as nonusers had in fact joined the program by the time that the groups were held. To the researchers' surprise, these mixed groups turned out to be extremely useful. The women who were still not using program wanted to hear why the new users had signed up for it, thus generating both penetrating questions from the nonusers as well as unsolicited testimonials from the new users. Since the research team's goal was to learn about the factors that would convert nonusers to new users, this was exactly the content that they wanted to hear!

EXAMPLE

Mixed Groups That Worked

What if you are unsure about whether to mix two potentially different categories of participants? The safest strategy in this case is to move from mixed to matched groups; that is, start with more broadly mixed groups, and then compose separate groups as you discover either concerns about incompatibility or categories of participants who are of special interest to you.

TIP

Starting With Mixed Groups Can Uncover Compatibility Issues

Segmentation: Comparing Categories of Participants

As we noted earlier in this chapter, segmentation is a strategy for dividing up the composition of a set of focus groups, such that each group is relatively homogeneous, while the full set of groups allows you to hear several potentially distinct perspectives. In the earlier discussion on the composition of individual focus groups, the emphasis was on the needs of the participants—especially the need to generate a good group dynamic by bringing together compatible participants. Here, the emphasis is on the researchers' concerns:

- Which particular categories of participants do you need to hear from?
- What kinds of similarities and differences do you need to understand?
- Who might be offended if you did not include them?

Using segmentation to determine the composition of focus groups means selecting carefully chosen categories of participants that fit your research purposes. Ideally, the decisions that you reach based on segmentation will match the decisions that you reach with regard to homogeneity and compatibility. In other words, the same factors that define a set of groups that interest you should also create compatible sets of participants. For example, in the previous section, we recommended separating users and nonusers of a product or service because of their potentially incompatible group dynamics; similarly, from a segmentation point of view, it is often desirable to separate users from nonusers so that you can systematically compare how these two segments respond to your interview questions.

There are numerous potential bases for segmentation, beginning with the same demographic characteristics that we considered as bases for homogeneity. With segmentation in mind, your research interests would lead you to make comparisons across groups that were separated according to gender, race or ethnicity, age, location, education, occupation or social class, income, marital status or family composition, and so on.

In thinking about demographic factors as a possible way to segment a set of groups into separate categories of participants, the key issue is whether the different demographic groups have different perspectives on the discussion topic(s). For example, if you are investigating factors that affect decisions about day care, the age and gender of the participants might not be as important as the differences between those with younger and older children or single mothers versus dual-career couples. What distinguishes these latter factors is that they directly affect how these categories of participants think about and experience the topic. Hence, you want to separate the participants into segments that are likely to correspond to different perspectives on the topic. In the day-care example, dual-career couples with preschool children may well have different perspectives from single mothers with older children. If both of these kinds of day-care decisions interested you, then you should segment the composition of your groups around these differences.

Beyond demographic characteristics, the next most common basis for segmentation is according to different experiences. Examples include the following:

- Users and nonusers for a product or service
- Those who are awaiting an experience and those who have already had it
- Those who occupy different social or organizational roles

Once again, the key assumption is that these different experiences will correspond to different perspectives on the topic. In some cases, this difference in perspectives may be the source of the experiences that you are examining. For example, what are the essential differences between the early and late adopters of an innovation? In other cases, the differences in perspective may be the result of differences in experiences. For example, among those who survive a wave of downsizing in a company, how do those who stay at their same jobs differ from those who must transfer to new positions?

Research sponsors are often interested in finding out more about those who do not use their products or services. Unfortunately, nonusers often lack interest in the topic, due to their lack of experience with it. This means that they may be difficult to recruit into the research in the first place. Then, even if they do show up, they may not have that much to say. When groups of nonusers are not only difficult to recruit but also yield unproductive discussions, the result is a deadly combination.

What if the research sponsors are committed to hearing from nonusers? The first thing to do is work with the sponsors to identify those segments of the nonusing population who are most likely to be interested in the project. Next, you need to find ways to get them into the group by maximizing their motivation, including the use of cash incentives if necessary. Finally, consider how to write interview questions that interest users and nonusers alike. The bottom line is that if you truly do want to work with nonusers, then you must allocate the effort this will take, both to recruit them and to generate an effective discussion.

Nonusers Can Be an Especially Difficult Segment

One final basis for segmenting categories of participants is according to differences in attitudes, opinions, and preferences. For example, imagine that you are designing a media campaign for a candidate in a close election. Often, the goal is to find messages that appeal to "swing voters," but it may be just as important to hold on to voters who currently favor your candidate. This would suggest segmenting the total set of groups so that some groups are composed of voters who are still undecided while other groups are composed of people who are "leaning toward" your candidate. Learning about the similarities in these two segments would help you appeal to both of them, while learning about their differences would help you avoid messages that might cost your candidate as much support as they produce.

Composing groups according to attitudes can be tricky, however, since those who share an opinion may have little else in common. The concern is that merely using attitudes to compose the groups may not be enough to spark a productive discussion. Worse still, these shared attitudes may bring together participants who are incompatible on other, more important bases. You can avoid these problems by ensuring that the attitudes in question are important to both the participants and the core topic of your research. When these two criteria are met, then you can be reasonably assured that the participants can maintain a civil discussion of the topics that interest you.

Using attitudes and opinions as the basis for segmentation also raises issues with regard to recruitment. When you are using segmentation, you have criteria for which participants fit into which groups. Typically, this involves asking questions during recruitment to screen for whether the participants have the desired characteristics. It is often easier to ask whether someone meets your recruiting criteria on demographic characteristics or prior experiences than it is to determine whether potential participants hold the appropriate attitudes and opinions. In some cases, you may end up doing the equivalent of a telephone survey just to locate people who hold the attitudes you are seeking.

Chapter 9 Discusses Screening During Recruitment

What If There Is One Major Category, but Others Also Matter?

Sometimes, there is one category of participants that matters the most, but other categories are also of interest. How do you divide the groups into segments when you are not equally interested in each category? One answer is to conduct multiple groups within the most important segment, compared to a single group in each of the other categories. This provides detailed data from the major category of participants while still allowing for comparisons between those participants and other potentially different types of participants.

This type of design often benefits from a flexible approach. For example, you might wait to conduct the final few groups with the majority category until after you have heard from the other sets of participants, so you can explore topics that come up in those other groups. Or, you might decide to conduct additional groups in a segment where you had initially only done one, so that you can learn more about this category of participants.

What if you are unsure about what segmentation strategy to use in determining the composition of a set of groups? In that case, it is wise to leave room to make adjustments. The easiest way to do this is to make sure, from the beginning, that your plans allow you the option to increase the number of groups. Sometimes, you learn that you need to include a new, additional segment. Sometimes, you learn that one of your original segments should really be subdivided into two separate sets of groups. Either of these contingencies will be much easier to meet if you have allowed for this possibility at the outset. For example, your budget might include a statement that "This project will have a minimum of 8 and possibly up to 12 groups," along with a consideration of the cost of these additional groups.

The value of this kind of flexibility is not limited to circumstances where you begin with some uncertainty about the composition of the groups. Even if you think you know what the basis for segmenting the groups will be, it is often advisable to leave room to modify or expand on your original choice of participants. You may well may change your mind about whom you need to hear from, depending on what you find along the way. Flexibility and openness are hallmarks of qualitative research, and a flexible approach can be especially important in decisions about group composition.

Allow for Flexibility in Decisions About Group Composition

Strangers or Acquaintances?

One final issue that arises with regard to group composition is whether the groups should be made up of strangers or acquaintances. Often, the real question is whether you have a choice. Those who routinely work with agencies and organizations frequently do not have the option of working with strangers. Imagine that you are conducting an evaluation with the employees of a organization that has just made major changes in its operating procedures. Unless this is a very large organization, it is inevitable that people who work together will know each other. This is not necessarily a disadvantage. These participants will all have gone through their experiences together, so they may be well prepared to discuss precisely the things that interest you.

In situations where you do have a choice between using strangers or acquaintances, the question becomes, What difference does it make? One obvious problem is that the presence of acquaintances limits confidentiality, since any information that participants share in the group can have later consequences. The main issue, however, is that strangers and acquaintances have different group dynamics. Some of these differences primarily affect the moderator's task in managing the group. Friends may "pair up," so that if one speaks, the other agrees. Alternatively, they may form a "conspiracy of silence," so that if one does not

The Focus Group Guidebook **Discusses Ethical Issues**

want to join in, the other will also hang back. Furthermore, if those who know each other sit together, they may break off into private conversations and asides, or they may just share glances and giggles that make others feel left out.

All of these issues can make a moderator's task more difficult, but the most important difference in group dynamics is that conversations among strangers avoid the taken for granted assumptions that are common among friends. Thus, statements that bring forth little more than a nod of agreement among friends may require considerable explanation to a group of strangers. If part of your purpose is to explore these kinds of "taken for granted assumptions," then a group of strangers will provide a more productive group dynamic.

The fact that strangers have to spend more time explaining themselves to each other is one reason that researchers who specialize in consumer products have such a strong preference for groups of strangers. When the goal is to learn how consumers' respond to products, you usually want a discussion that will give you as much detail and insight into this process as possible. In fact, you might be most interested in the very things that friends would take for granted about each others' experiences and preferences. For projects where the goals are similar to this kind of product marketing, it can make sense to take advantage of this aspect of the group dynamics among strangers. For projects with different purposes, however, there may be little reason to worry about whether participants are acquaintances or strangers.

Putting It Together: Group Composition Affects Other Decisions

Decisions about who the participants are typically get made very early in the planning for a focus group project. Both creating homogeneous groups and segmenting groups may require adjustments in other procedures. Whenever a project involves different categories of participants, this will affect many of the other aspects of research.

Recruiting is the most obvious task that depends on group composition, and many of the issues in Chapter 9 are a direct continuation of themes that arise here. In some respects, the difference between that chapter and this is largely a matter of emphasis. While this chapter considers the broad issues, that one concentrates on the mechanics of locating the appropriate participants and getting them to the group.

Writing questions for the interview also depends on the group composition, since good questions will take into account who is in each group and how similar the groups are to each another. If you wish to make effective comparisons across a set of groups, then the questions need to be reasonably similar from group to group. And, when you are working with different groups, your questions need to be equally appropriate for everyone.

Moderators need to know about any differences in the composition of the groups they will work with. Knowing about differences up front will allow them to think through the tension between maintaining consistency across groups and adjusting their style to take into account differences between groups.

Analysis techniques also need to be sensitive to any differences in group composition. At a minimum, the analyst must be able to make comparisons across different categories of participants. In addition, when you are working with mixed groups, the analyst needs to know who was in which category.

BACKGROUND

Should the Moderator Be Like the Participants?

In bringing together decisions about who the participants should be and who the moderator(s) should be, there is often a question about the extent to which the moderator's characteristics should match those of the participants. Some sources insist that moderators should always match participants; for example, only females should moderate groups of women, only African Americans should moderate groups of blacks, and so forth. We prefer a less rigid approach that focuses on how the match between the moderator and the participants will affect the discussion, which is, after all, the point of the group.

In some cases, it may be that a group of participants will feel comfortable only when they are with a moderator they perceive as compatible. For example, race is such a pervasive issue in American society that most projects that conduct separate groups by race may want to consider finding matching moderators, even if the discussion does not have an overtly racial theme.

In other cases, a moderator who is distinctly different from the participants may have advantages. Taking on the role of a stranger allows such a moderator to ask questions that might seem silly coming from a fellow member of the category. It is unwise to carry this pose of naïveté or ignorance to an extreme, but it can create an opportunity to ask some very basic questions.

Another argument against rigid matching is that there are many instances where it would be quite absurd. If you were interested in the environmental knowledge of 7-year olds, you would not want a second grader to moderate the group. Furthermore, if you were to carry the logic of moderator matching to an extreme, you might need a different moderator for every group.

Ultimately, the question of whether the moderator should match the participants is an extension of the basic question about who the participants should be: Will these participants feel comfortable discussing this topic, not only among themselves but with this moderator?

7

Deciding on Group Size

We've all been in groups that were so large that only the most forceful people could get their ideas heard, or groups that were so small that we felt compelled to contribute just to keep things going. Focus groups are the same: Size matters. Deciding on the right number of participants for a focus group means striking a balance between having enough people to generate a discussion and not having so many people that some feel crowded out. Groups of six to ten usually accomplish this, but there are several situations where a smaller or larger group is more likely to lead to success.

Typical Group Size Is Six to Ten

For most purposes, six participants would be considered a relatively small focus group, while ten would be a relatively large one. This size range provides enough different opinions to stimulate a discussion without making each participant compete for time to talk.

Unfortunately, simply selecting a size of six to ten participants is too vague for most purposes. Effective planning means thinking about the differences between smaller and larger groups. Smaller groups give each participant a greater opportunity to talk, but they also place a greater burden on each person to carry the conversation. How much does the research topic interest these participants—would six of them really have enough to say about each question to keep the ball rolling? If not, avoid smaller groups. By comparison, large groups place less responsibility on each participant, but they also provide less opportunity to talk. Would ten of these participants have enough time to say everything they had to say about this topic? If not, avoid larger groups.

In making decisions about group size, it is useful to think concretely about how much time each participant will get to talk in the group. For example, most focus groups last 90 minutes, so eight participants would get just over 10 minutes apiece during the whole group. If the interview guide calls for 10 questions, then each person gets only one minute per question! And that doesn't consider the fact that the moderator will be speaking for part of the time.

BACKGROUND

**How Much
Time to Talk?**

Calculating how much time the average participant gets to discuss a question depends on three things:

1. How many participants there are (typically, 6 to 10)

2. How many questions there are (typically, 8 to 12)

3. How long the group lasts (typically, 1 to 2 hours)

The three options in this table show the two extremes and the mid-range.

Number of Participants	Number of Questions	Group Length in Minutes	Minutes per Person per Question
6	8	120	2.5
8	10	90	1.1
10	12	60	0.5

The first option demonstrates that it is possible to hear a fair amount from each participant by using smaller groups, fewer questions, and more time. The middle option is the source of the guideline that each participant will typically get one minute per question. At the upper extreme, it is hard to imagine any practical reason for cramming together so many people and to discuss so many questions in such a short a time.

Many people are concerned the first time they realize that many focus groups give each participant an average of only one minute per question. The reality, however, is that some participants will have more to say about any question and others will have less to say. There is no point in metering each participant's contribution to each question, as long as there is no tendency for a few participants to dominate the whole discussion. The goal should be to inspire a lively discussion of each question so that those who are most interested get the chance to tell their story.

Of course, a lot depends on the participants you get in any particular group. A small group with three or four outspoken individuals can be difficult to control, and a large group made up entirely of timid talkers may fall flat. The impossibility of predicting the dynamics of any given group is not, however, an excuse for ignoring those dynamics. Planning to bring together the right number of participants is an important element in producing effective discussions.

When to Use Smaller Groups

The most obvious reason for using groups of six or fewer is that each participant has a lot to say. Having fewer participants gives each one more time to tell personal stories or express heartfelt opinions. Often, this matches a project goal of getting a more in-depth understanding of what participants have to say.

- When participants have a high level of involvement with the topic
- When participants are emotionally caught up in the topic
- When the participants are experts or know a lot about the topic
- When the topic is controversial
- When the topic is complex
- When the goal is to hear detailed stories and personal accounts
- When recruitment factors limit other options

Reasons for Using Smaller Groups

The concept of *higher involvement* is a general summary of situations where the participants have strong feelings about the topic. This goes beyond simply having a lot to say about it. Highly involved participants will get frustrated if they are cut off before they say everything they have to say; smaller groups increase their opportunity to express themselves fully. Strong feelings about a topic can also produce strong reactions to what others say. The

The Focus Group Guidebook Discusses the Ethics of Self-Disclosure

more intimate setting of a small group lets participants get to know each other, and this smooths the way for the give-and-take of a more intense discussion.

Emotionally charged topics offer the clearest example of high involvement, and smaller groups are by far the safest approach to emotional topics. Dealing with fewer participants allows the moderator to pay more attention to each one's needs. In addition, hearing more from the other members of the group lets each participant get to know the others better. This allows all participant to gauge an appropriate level of self-disclosure about their own experiences and feelings.

Controversial topics also benefit from the deeper acquaintance that develops in smaller groups. Giving participants the chance to get to know each other as fully rounded individuals is more likely to create the climate of mutual respect that is necessary for airing controversy. Of course, this has to be matched by an interviewing strategy that starts by exploring easier topics and then builds to the tougher issues after the participants are indeed familiar with each other.

In addition to giving each participant more opportunity to participate, smaller groups also allow the research team to hear more from each participant. Smaller groups offer a distinct advantage when it is important to learn more about each participant's experiences or thoughts. For example, we used groups of participants in a study of why families had sought a diagnosis for Alzheimer's disease (which was presented as an example of a highly structured group in Chapter 5). We began by asking each participant about the first symptom that indicated that his or her family member had a memory problem. After each person had a chance to tell this part of the story, we followed through with other experiences, question by question (e.g., how had things changed since those first symptoms appeared, when did someone first talk to a doctor). Limiting the group size allowed us to hear a relatively detailed history of what happened in each family.

Occasionally, a small group is the only possible option. There may be only a few eligible participants, or it may be difficult to schedule more than a handful of appropriate people to be in the same place at the same time. In this case, it is important to remember the responsibility that a smaller group puts on each person to participate. If the participants are highly involved with the topic, this is not a problem. If their involvement level is low, however, it may be necessary to modify the questions to encourage more participation. As a final fall back, you may have to accept the fact that a small group discussing a low-involvement topic will run short. If the participants do not have much to say, that fact can be useful data in itself.

Developing Questions for Focus Groups Describes Ways to Generate Active Participation

I once conducted a group of three people composed of two CEOs from large firms and a third participant who was a recognized expert on the topic. They had all participated in a variety of task forces related to the topic, so they each had quite a lot to say, along with detailed reactions to each others' ideas. Not only was this small group very productive, but the 90 minutes went by incredibly quickly. Adding even one more participant would have increased the frustration level of all.

EXAMPLE

When Only a Small Group Will Do

When to Use Larger Groups

The factors that encourage the use of larger groups are basically the reverse of those that may make small groups desirable.

TIP

- *When participants have a low level of involvement with the topic*
- *When the goal is to hear numerous brief suggestions, as in brainstorming*
- *When recruitment factors limit other options*

Reasons for Using Larger Groups

Low-involvement topics often lead to the decision to use groups with 10 or more participants. When most participants will have little to say about any given question, having more participants multiplies the chance that someone will readily respond to each question. Once the ball starts rolling, a larger group also makes it more likely that someone will react to whatever is said.

- Maybe someone has had a similar experience.
- Maybe someone tried the same approach, but it didn't work for her.
- Maybe someone used to think that but now has changed his mind.

With any luck, a larger group will produce both the initial responses and the follow-up reactions that lead to a lively discussion.

TIP

The participation of "nonusers" in a focus group represents a case where low levels of involvement are especially likely to be a problem. What do people who never use a service or a product have to say about it? Yet, these nonusers are often a crucial target audience. Plan for larger groups when talking to nonusers. This makes it more likely that their limited individual experiences will fit together in an effective group discussion.

Consider Using Larger Groups When Talking to "Nonusers"

**A Lively
Discussion of a
Low-Involvement
Topic**

How much could you say about bar soap? I once watched a marketing researcher use this very topic in a demonstration group with a dozen professors and graduate students. The first question was, "Where in your house do you have soap?" This was something that everyone could answer, and it led to a mental scavenger hunt as the participants tried to think of all the places where they had soap. Later questions included, "Let's just think about the bathroom; what kinds of soap do you have there?" and "Who in your family uses these different kinds of soaps?" Each question easily sparked a response from someone and then multiple reactions around the table. Some liked soaps with cleansing cream in them, others preferred soaps with deodorant, and still others wanted soap that was "pure." One person used dishwashing liquid for all his personal hygiene needs, while another's husband relied exclusively on the miniature bars of soap that he brought home from motels. In the end, this group of intellectuals was astonished at how much they had enjoyed talking about such a seemingly mundane topic.

Unless you reduce the number of questions or increase the time length, a larger group inherently means hearing less from each participant. Sometimes, this is desirable. When the goal of the group is brainstorming or generating ideas, brief suggestions may be exactly right. There is a danger, however, that a larger group will cause these discussions to get out of hand, especially with higher levels of involvement. One way to solve this problem is to encourage each participant to contribute several separate ideas to each discussion point. This strategy is sometimes referred to as "popcorning," since it aims to get a steady series of short bursts of participation around the table.

Finally, there is the case when the realities of recruiting make a large group the only option. This is especially likely to happen with preexisting groups. On occasion, it may be possible to take along more than one moderator and split up such a group. More often, it is necessary to make accommodations by adapting the interview questions and moderating strategy.

**A Large
Preexisting
Group**

I once conducted a focus group with 19 staff members of a large nursing home to discuss their relations with their patients' families. Given the staff's complex schedules, their regular staff meeting was the only time that any substantial number of them could get together. Fortunately, the self-imposed discipline that they used to conduct orderly staff meetings carried over into a well-functioning group discussion. Furthermore, each was quite interested in the topic and equally interested in hearing what others had to say.

One useful strategy in this situation was to take advantage of the fact that the participants all knew a great deal about each other. This made them very responsive to requests about "who else" had something to say on a given topic. For example, a probe about "Who else hears complaints from patients' families?" led several participants to glance toward the head of maintenance. He then explained that he lived on the grounds, so on weekends, he was often the most senior staff member that families could find.

8

Deciding on the Number of Groups

Overview

Typical Number of Groups Is Three to Five
When Are More Groups Necessary?
When Are Fewer Groups Acceptable?
Using Just One Group Is Often Risky

There is no hard-and-fast rule about how many focus groups are enough. Doing too few groups may miss something or lead to premature conclusions, but doing too many is obviously a waste of time and money. Planning ahead will certainly help, but flexibility can be even more important. Sometimes, the only way to find out if a project requires either more groups or fewer groups is to try it and find out.

Typical Number of Groups Is Three to Five

Deciding on the right number of groups is a matter of hearing what there is to hear. If practically everyone has the same thoughts on a topic, this will be evident after a few groups. When the responses are more diverse, it will take considerably more groups to hear what people have to say. Thus, the biggest issue in determining the number of groups is the underlying diversity in what people have to say.

The idea that most projects require three to five groups assumes that the participants are only moderately diverse and that the topic is only moderately complex. When this is true, there is a diminishing return for each additional group that you conduct. That is, the third group will add less new information than the second group, and the fourth group will add still less. By the end of a long series of groups, you often have the impression that you know everything that participants have to say. Sometimes, as soon as one person says one thing, you know exactly how the next person is going to respond. When the groups become repetitive, you have reached a point of "theoretical saturation," and there is little to be gained by doing more groups.

BACKGROUND

Theoretical Saturation

Theoretical saturation is a basic concept in qualitative research. It was first introduced by Glaser and Strauss. Basically, theoretical saturation is a process of adding cases (in this case, focus groups) until you have uncovered the full range of what there is to observe. The actual number of cases is less important than the sense of having fully covered or saturated the topic of study. Saturation is achieved when new cases no longer yield new information. (Glaser & Strauss, 1967)

In most cases, it is difficult to anticipate exactly how many groups it will take to reach saturation. All the same, it is not that hard to distinguish between projects that are likely to require either more or fewer groups. The topic for the project is a major factor. Is this a complex topic that raises different issues for different people? Then it is likely to require more groups in order to hear all that the various participants have to say. The number of groups also depends on the project's goals. Is this exploratory research, where it is uncertain what people will have to say? Then it may well take a larger number of groups to uncover this information.

BACKGROUND

Sample Size in Qualitative and Quantitative Research

In social science research, the amount of data that is necessary depends in large part on the diversity of the people being studied. Quantitative methods build this variability into the statistical formulas that guide their procedures. In survey research, the variance in the population is a major influence on sample size. In experimental research, the variance in the population influences the relationship between the number of subjects and the power of statistical tests.

In qualitative research, there are no precise formulas, but the basic issue is the same. Trying to understand a more diverse population means conducting more focus groups— or individual interviews or case studies. This follows directly from the principle of theoretical saturation, since it will take longer to achieve a sense of completion or repetition when there are more points of views to hear.

When Are More Groups Necessary?

Plan to use more groups whenever there is a diverse range of responses to a topic. When participants have many different experiences or opinions, it takes more groups to hear what they have to say. For focus groups, dealing with diversity goes beyond the need to work with more people in order to hear their different points of view. Working with groups adds an extra dimension.

Each group's discussion is influenced by the particular mix of opinions and experiences that its particular participants bring to it. For example, even if the broader population's thoughts about some issue are split 50/50, it is unlikely that a focus group with eight people in it will have four in favor of the issue and four opposed. A group that is split five to three in favor of the issue may well have different discussion from one that is split five to three against it. Furthermore, there may be many reasons to be either for or against a particular issue, so it can take several groups to hear them all.

The project's goals may also lead to the decision to use more groups. Having more groups does more than just reveal the range of diversity in what people have to say. Having more groups also yields insights into the sources and comparisons across groups.

- Why do some people have one experience while others have another?
- Who thinks what?
- What makes a difference?

Jenny Kitzinger conducted a study that used preliminary focus groups to help generate the content for a media project on AIDS in Great Britain. She and her colleagues conducted 52 groups with 351 participants. Why were so many groups necessary?

- *The topic was complex, and the researchers wanted to know as much as possible about not just what people thought but why they thought that way.*

EXAMPLE

A Very Large Project

> • *The project operated throughout the country and covered a wide range of different perspectives. Some of the groups were drawn from the general population; others tapped into special perspectives, such as those of prison officers, male prostitutes, intravenous drug users, and lesbians.*
>
> *Hearing about a wide range of issues from a wide range of perspectives led to the need for a very large number of groups. Fortunately, this project was funded by a government grant that made it possible not only to collect these data but also to process and analyze them. (Kitzinger, 1994)*

Chapter 6 Discusses Segmentation

When participants have many different experiences or opinions, it is often advisable to adjust the group composition, as discussed in Chapter 6, so that separate groups represent distinct segments. Be aware, however, that using segments will increase the number of groups. If the goal is to compare separate segments of men and women, or younger and older people, or those in different regions, then there have to be enough groups *within each segment*. Once again, this is a matter of hearing what there is to hear, but now, there have to be enough groups to hear what each segment has to say. For example, if a new program will serve several different categories of clients, then it is advisable to learn how participants from each category respond to the proposed program. If it takes three to five groups to hear what the participants in any one segment have to say, then a comparison across segments will automatically multiply the total number of groups.

Of course, more is not always better. The obvious problem with conducting a large number of groups is that the process is expensive and time-consuming. The less obvious problem is that it can greatly complicate analysis. Often, the analytic process involves making comparisons across all the groups in a set. This is relatively straightforward when there are three to five groups in a set. When there are a dozen or more groups in a set, however, making systematic comparisons is extremely demanding. Is Group 4 more like Group 6 or Group 9? Is the way that Group 3 differs from Group 1 the same as the way that it differs from Group 8? Mathematically speaking, increases in the number of groups lead to a geometric growth in the number of comparisons. For example, a set of 5 groups generates 10 possible pairwise comparisons, while a set of 10 groups generates 45 such pairings. If this technical explanation does not convince you of the complexity of analyzing a large number of focus groups, then talk to someone who has tried it!

Analyzing and Reporting Focus Group Results Discusses Group-to-Group Comparisons

What if a project involves the need to hear from several different segments, but there are tight limits on time or money? Inevitably, something has to give somewhere. Still, there are some things you can do.

When Multiple Segments Put a Strain on Resources

- *Use fewer segments. Decide which differences in the population really require attention at this time. Don't divide the groups into segments that you don't really need. For example, some researchers automatically use separate groups of men and women, but are sex differences really relevant for your particular project?*

- *Don't feel compelled to use the same number of groups in every segment. One strategy is to start with two groups in each segment and then follow up with a few more groups in the segments where the initial responses were most complex or diverse.*

When Are Fewer Groups Acceptable?

The safest reason for using fewer groups is a lack of diversity in responses. If the discussions reach saturation and become repetitive after two or three groups, there is little to be gained by doing more. For some topics, hearing what there is to hear may not take many groups. One classic example involves institutional food in school cafeterias, college dorms, and so forth. Just how wide is the range of opinions on this topic?

The problem for planning is that it is difficult to know in advance how variable opinions and experiences will be. When the degree of diversity is open to question, it is better to err on the side of having too many groups rather than too few. Having too many groups is merely inefficient—the last ones will be repetitive. Having too few groups leaves many unknowns. It is frustrating to walk away from a research project with more questions and fewer answers. In addition, discovering that the project plan did not include enough groups can lead to embarrassing requests for a larger budget and longer timelines. By contrast, finding out that the project can be done with fewer groups than planned may generate cost savings and early delivery.

What If You Have More Groups Scheduled Than You Need?

Sometimes it isn't possible to cancel the rest of the groups, even if they are becoming repetitive. In some cases, there may be contracts either with outside moderators or for the rental of special facilities. In other cases, it may be difficult to ask the remaining participants not to attend, especially if they have some ongoing relationship with the organization sponsoring the project.

In these circumstances, reconsider the original project goals to find a creative use for the remaining groups.

- *Are there new questions to ask? Perhaps the earlier groups provided clues about issues that were not anticipated when the original questions were written.*
- *Are there new categories of participants to hear from? Perhaps the responses in the earlier groups highlighted the distinctive perspectives of certain groups, indicating the need to hear from a new segment.*
- *Did the first set of groups identify a set of problems? If so, you can conduct a second wave of groups to seek solution strategies.*
- *Is it important to verify the results? If so, you can use an additional set of groups as a sounding board to react to your tentative conclusions.*

Using Just One Group Is Often Risky

When the data have come from just one group, it is impossible to separate the content of the discussion from what was unique about that group. Many things can influence what was said during the discussion in any given group.

- Maybe the composition of this group was unbalanced.

    Were they mostly women?

    Did they have an unusually high level of education?

- Maybe these participants had an odd mix of personalities.

    Did one pair of participants seem to become instant best friends?

    Was there someone who seemed to irritate everyone else?

- Maybe the group dynamics were unusual in other ways.

    Did a few talkative participants dominate the discussion?

    Did a feud break out at some point?

Analyzing and Reporting Focus Group Results Discusses Group-to-Group Comparisons

Imagine that all you have is the transcript from a single focus group. What are you to make of these data? Does the discussion represent what most people like this have to say about this topic? Or is it just what this unique group of people had to say to each other at this particular time? With just one group, there is no way to know.

The advantage of having several groups is most evident during the analysis of the data. When analyzing focus groups, making comparisons across multiple groups provides a better sense of which topics are most important. Each individual group will have some things that it emphasizes more than the others do. Having several groups to compare reveals which issues are specific to a single group and which ones come up repeatedly.

Often, the person who commissioned the research is the source of the suggestion to do only one group. Managers are often most concerned about the time and cost of research. Researchers, however, are always sensitive to the quality of the data, especially if it influences decision making.

What is a researcher to do if a manager wants to rely on just one group? The simplest suggestion is to ask for a minimum of two groups. If both groups basically agree, this greatly reduces the chance that their shared message was due to a chance mix of personalities or group dynamics. If the two groups disagree, the lack of a shared message will deter using either group as a narrow basis for decision making.

TIP

Two Groups Are Much Better Than One

Does this mean that no one should ever use just one group? No. The heading for this section says that using just one group is risky, not wrong. Sometimes there are simply not enough participants in the whole world for two groups, or it would be too expensive and time-consuming to assemble multiple groups. In those cases, it may make sense to conduct a single group, so long as the data are interpreted cautiously. Once again, the crucial limitation is that the content of the discussion cannot be separated from either the unique characteristics of the participants or their group dynamics. Any project that relies on just one group must explicitly confront this limitation.

Comparing data from two different sources is known as "triangulation." When you have only one focus group, triangulation can help you determine whether the content of that discussion is consistent with information from other sources.

BACKGROUND

Triangulation Can Help

- *Have others conducted surveys or done observations?*
- *Are there records or archives with relevant information?*
- *Can key informants comment on the same issues?*

The value of triangulation goes well beyond studies that use only one focus group. For example, whenever there are inconsistencies in the data, no matter how many groups you have done, comparisons to other sources can help. For projects that involve important decisions or sensitive issues, it is often wise to rely on more than one type of data.

9

Recruiting the Participants

Overview

What Is the Source of the Participants?
Making Contact
Screening Finds Special Categories of Participants
Giving and Receiving Information
Incentives Encourage Participation
Timing and Location Make a Difference
Plan Ahead to Minimize No-Show Rates
Professional Recruiting Services Are an Option
Checklist for Successful Recruitment
Examples of Recruitment Scripts

When too few people show up, your focus group is an outright failure. All the effort and expense that went into writing the questions, training the moderator, and contacting the participants is wasted. Fortunately, this problem can be avoided through careful planning in the recruitment stages of the project. Recruitment may be the least glamorous aspect of focus groups, but it is absolutely essential to their success.

Recruitment is a systematic process. The traditional three-step strategy for recruitment includes the following: Two weeks before the actual group, you should make contact with the participants. One week before, they should receive a confirma-

Chapter 6
Discusses
Decisions About
Who the
Participants
Should Be

tion letter from you. The day before the group, you should make a follow-up phone call to every participant.

Yet, the first step in recruitment actually begins before a single telephone call is made. This is when you decide which people to recruit. The basic rule is that you must know whom to recruit before you can decide *how* to recruit them. Chapter 6 discussed the general principles that determine the composition of focus groups. This chapter will continue that discussion by considering the mechanics of locating the people you want and ensuring that they will attend the actual focus groups.

What Is the Source of the Participants?

There are many potential sources for locating participants. These include existing lists, random sampling, referrals, intercepts, and open solicitation.

Existing Lists. The most common starting point for recruitment is a list of potential participants. If you have already made the decision about whom the participants will be, your next step will often be to locate lists of those potential participants. It can be tempting just to use a convenient list for your recruitment; you must be careful, however, that the people on the list actually match your needs.

The goal of recruitment is to make sure that enough of the right people actually show up for the focus groups. Using a convenient list may help you get enough people, but will they be the right people? Successful recruitment is not just a matter of numbers; otherwise, you could just drag people in off the streets. As Chapter 6 emphasized, decisions about the composition of focus groups involve both how comfortable the participants will be with each other and how productive their discussion will be. So, the success of both the individual groups and the project as a whole depends on recruiting the right participants.

Suppose you do have a list of potential participants. How might you evaluate it? Ask yourself:

- What is the source of the list?
- How recent is the list?
- How detailed is the information in the list?
- Does it mix together people you want to recruit and people you do not?

Of course, the optimum is to recruit from a source that adds credibility to your contacts while providing up-to-date and detailed information on exactly the people you want. In reality, the quality of lists varies widely. Sometimes, you have no more than a collection of names, without so much as a telephone number or an address. If this is the best you can do, it will at least get you started looking in phone books, city directories, and so on. At the other extreme, you might have access to a full database that includes a great deal more than just the basic contact information. That additional information can be quite useful, since it allows you to be much more selective in your recruiting. Perhaps you are seeking families with young children: Does the list contain information about who has children and their ages, or will you have to call through the entire list and ask each person you reach?

Aside from the raw information in a list, its next most important characteristic is its source. Lists often signal relationships. The very existence of the list tells you something about the relationship between the people on the list and the source of your list. This is true for lists of members in nonprofit organizations, clients of government agencies, and business customers. When you contact people, they will often want to know how you got their names. If the list that put you in touch is part of a positive, ongoing relationship that an individual has with some group or organization, this can be a tremendous aid.

If you do not already have a list, the question is how you can find one. The most straightforward strategy is to rely on key informants and relevant organizations. Who can tell you where to find the kinds of participants you need? Some groups make their membership lists available as a fund-raiser, so you might be able to do your recruitment that way. For example, if you want to interview baby boomers, you might be able to find them through any number of volunteer organizations (although using just a single source, such as members of a particular church, might well skew your sample).

When you are working with members of the general population, it is possible to purchase lists from a variety of sources, including utility companies, the bureau of motor vehicles, or the board of elections. For example, in a study that we did on retirees who had moved into an area, the local phone company sold us a list of all their customers who had started new phone service during the past 5 years and were over the age of 60. Any large city is likely to have companies that prepare and sell lists from these sources, so check under "Mailing Lists" in the Yellow Pages. There are also various national services that can often create such lists for specific local areas.

Marketing research firms that do recruitment for focus groups often have lists of prior participants. The advantage of these lists is that they consist of people who have been through

The Focus Group Guidebook Discusses Relationships Between Sponsors and Participants

Single Sources of Lists Can Skew Results

the process before, so it is usually easier to reach them and get a quick answer about their willingness to participate in a new group. The disadvantage is that the people on these lists may have quite a few assumptions about what focus groups are and how they should behave in them. Indeed, the fact that commercial recruiting sources routinely pay people $35 to $50 to participate in a focus group means that they sometimes acquire a stable of "focus groupies"—people who participate in groups because they enjoy either the money or the discussions.

To get around the problem of repeat participants, some researchers have attempted to use people who have never been in a focus group before; however, with the increasing popularity of focus groups, this can become difficult to do. The obvious question here is whether a participant's prior experience with focus groups makes any difference for your research purposes. In the example where you are trying to recruit baby boomers, you probably don't care what other kinds of focus groups these people have participated in before. But if you are working on an election campaign, you almost certainly want people who are interested in discussing the specific issues that matter to you, not those who are trying to get into any and every focus group.

Random Sampling. As we discussed in Chapter 6 of this volume, true random samples are seldom used in focus group research. Once again, however, it is important not to confuse random sampling with randomizing the choice of names from an existing list in order to eliminate bias in selection procedures.

Chapter 6 Discusses Random Sampling and Focus Groups

When you truly need random sampling, you can recruit focus group participants in many of the same ways that survey researchers locate their respondents. For focus groups, the most common of these approaches is through random digit dialing (RDD). Although the actual use of RDD usually involves sophisticated computer-assisted interviewing, the concept itself is quite simple. You simply generate random lists of potential phone numbers and call until you locate enough participants. The obvious strength of this system is that it gets around unlisted numbers, which constitute more than 20% of the residential listings in some areas. The more sophisticated, computer-based RDD systems can also get around some of the disadvantages in this process, such as phone numbers that do not actually exist, and business listings.

Any form of random sampling to obtain specific categories of participants is essentially a hit-and-miss process, so the obvious question is: What is your likely hit rate? As a general rule, random sampling is most viable when you are searching for participants with relatively common characteristics. If you are seeking out rare populations, you may have to make quite a few calls before you reach a potentially eligible participant. In that case, an existing list would provide a much higher hit rate, but at the cost of losing the representativeness that goes with random sampling. Projects that require random samples of rare populations had better have very large recruitment budgets!

Referrals. Other people can often be your best source of potential participants. Key informants can be a crucial source of contacts, allowing you to reach one person who produces several names, rather than hunting those names down, one at a time. Snowball sampling is another popular form of recruitment through referrals. Snowball sampling refers to the process of asking people you have already recruited for the names of other potential participants—the analogy is thus to a process where a small snowball grows as it rolls downhill. Snowball sampling takes advantage of social networks, so locating one person who fits your recruitment criteria may provide connections to others whom that person knows. For example, I was recently recruited to participate in a focus group for people who have color printers, based on a referral from a friend who had been contacted to participate but did not own that particular piece of computer equipment.

Because groups that occur in the workplace involve time off from the job, work supervisors are often used as a referral source to select participants. If you use this approach, you will need to monitor this process so the supervisors don't handpick the participants. If possible, provide a list of the people you would like as potential participants and let the supervisors select from this list. At a minimum, provide clear screening criteria for who is eligible to participate and politely let the supervisors know that you will double-check the recruitment criteria when the participants arrive.

Referrals in Work Settings Can Cause Problems

Intercepts. Intercepts are based on finding the participants at a location where the focus group will be held. One common form of intercept sampling occurs in shopping malls. If a mall includes a focus group facility, then it is possible to intercept shoppers and invite them into a group that will be starting almost immediately. A recruiter, typically armed with a clipboard, approaches people who appear to meet a set of criteria (e.g., women aged 35 to 50) and asks them a few questions to determine whether they are suitable for the focus group (e.g., if they use the type of consumer products that will be the subject of the discussion). When people meet the recruiting criteria, the recruiter typically offers them an incentive in return for joining a group that is about to begin.

Intercepts are not limited to malls with specialized facilities. They can be an especially useful recruitment strategy at recreation areas and other gathering places. Meetings and conferences are other settings where it is possible to intercept people who fit your required criteria. The strategy here is to take advantage of an occasion that brings together a concentrated group of potential participants and then to recruit them into a group that will be happening on-site. This is sometimes referred to as "piggybacking" a focus group onto another event.

The obvious advantage of intercepts as a recruitment strategy is that they bring the focus group to the participants. The corresponding weakness is that they requires people to fit the focus group in with what they are already doing. For intercepts to work, participating in the group has to fit in with what people are already doing in the setting where you intercept them. At meetings and conferences, this is often accomplished by pairing the group discussion with a private dinner that is held outside other scheduled activities.

For meetings where you know in advance who will be attending, you can modify the intercept approach by contacting potential participants before the meeting to schedule them into a group that will not conflict with the meeting itself. For example, we recruited a group of doctors by inviting them to a buffet meal and focus group that we held at their local medical association, right before the regularly scheduled monthly meeting.

Open Solicitation. Another popular way to locate focus group participants is to advertise for them. Newspapers are the most common way to solicit participants, but bulletin boards, newsletters, and broadcast media all present opportunities. In each of these cases, the potential participant responds to some kind of public notice or announcement.

The most likely use for this recruitment strategy occurs when you are seeking a particular category of participants but do not have a list or any other resources for locating the people you need. The danger in using advertisements is that the participants will be self-selected. Out of all of the people who encounter a public notice, which ones will actually respond? One way to deal with this problem is to compare groups that you recruit through open solicitations with groups that you draw from other sources. For example, in working with a local neighborhood association to help set its future policies, we compared people who had already contacted the association about their interest in this topic with other groups that we recruited by telephone. As it turned out, the self-selected participants had a distinctly different agenda from the ordinary neighborhood residents.

As this last example illustrates, recruitment can have a major influence on what you learn from your focus groups. Whatever your source of participants, the bottom line is that you need a systematic, well-described recruitment process. To evaluate your recruitment plans, try some role playing.

EXERCISE

Defending Recruitment Procedures

Imagine that you are making an oral presentation of your final report, and someone important asks you, "Just where did you find these people? Why should we pay any attention to what they have to say?" How will you answer these questions? How will you defend your choices about which people to interview? How will you describe the procedures that you used to find them? In short, how will you convince your audience that you used a sound strategy to locate the right people to talk to?

Making Contact

Setting up effective contact and recruitment procedures requires a careful planning effort and foresight. Before you make your first contact, you have to know what you will say, and you have to have thought through the various contingencies you are likely to encounter.

In order to convince people to participate in a focus group, you have to understand why you are contacting them. In almost every case, the basic reason that you are contacting them is that you want to hear from them and others like them. So, the fundamental message is that they have a point of view that is important to you. The best way to get this message across is, once again, to do some role playing. Imagine that you were this participant receiving this recruitment contact.

- What would matter to you?
- What would you want to know?
- What would encourage you to react more favorably to this request?
- What would convince you that it was important to participate in this project?

**Recruiting
Participants
Differs From
Recruiting
Volunteers**

Some organizations have strategies for recruiting volunteers that may be less appropriate for recruiting focus group participants. True, you are asking people for their help when you ask them to participate in a focus group, but the real issue in recruiting for focus groups is getting the categories of people that you need for this project. For most focus groups, you do not want just the most active or most accessible members of an organization, but these are precisely the people who are most likely to be volunteers. So, if you are working with an organization that routinely uses volunteers, you may want to warn them up front that their usual procedures for getting volunteers are not likely to produce the right participants for focus groups.

Setting up your recruitment procedures also means giving attention to who will be doing the recruiting. Your recruiters need to have both the professional know-how necessary to implement your procedures and the people skills necessary to make a favorable impression on the people they talk to. Depending on the complexity of your recruitment process, there may be a considerable training period prior to launching the full-scale operation.

**Recruitment
Requires Either
Skill or Training**

From an organizational and financial point of view, it is often tempting to use your existing staff as the recruitment team. Whether this is really a practical strategy depends on both which people you are recruiting and how much training your staff will need.

When you are recruiting participants who have an ongoing relationship with your organization, using your existing staff to contact them can really save money. When you are recruiting people who do not know you or your organization, however, using available staff and volunteers may not be a cost-effective strategy. Often, untrained recruiters have a much lower "hit rate," so they need to make considerably more contacts in order to get someone to agree to participate.

If you do use your own people as the recruitment team, then it is essential that you train and monitor them. Do not assume that prior experience in dealing with the public over the telephone is sufficient. Make sure that your staff or volunteers understand what they are asking people to do and that they feel confident in conveying the importance of participating in these focus groups. If your staff members are not well trained in recruitment skills, you may be setting them up for the thoroughly frustrating experience of making many calls with little to show for it.

Finally, before you assume that your staff members are indeed available to do the recruitment, remember that the prime calling times for recruitment are typically in the early evening, well after regular working hours. Hence, there can also be logistical barriers to using existing staff.

Timing is a crucial part of making contact. Consider the people you want to contact, and ask yourself when you can reach them. Commercial recruitment firms consider the hours between

6:00 and 8:00 on weekday evenings to be the prime time for telephone contacts, but this might not be the best time for the specific people you are seeking. If you are working with retirees, making contact calls during the late morning or early afternoon might be the most convenient time for both of you. Plus, there is always the consideration that some people don't like to be disturbed during the dinner hour. Just because people are likely to be home at certain times does not mean that they want to talk to a focus group recruiter then!

As you plan your contact procedures, be sure to spend some time thinking about which people these procedures might be missing. This is especially important in setting up telephone contact procedures. Often, telephones are the only practical means for recruiting, but you still need to consider who might not be reachable by phone. If you are working through published directories, you will not get unlisted numbers, which typically represent an upper-income group. There may be some types of participants who are not available during the hours when you are calling. For example, many professionals, such as doctors and teachers, are difficult to contact by telephone during their working hours, and some low-income participants will not have phones at all. For categories of potential participants who cannot be reached over the phone, the only alternative may be in-person contacts, such as intercepts at meetings or other gatherings.

Anyone who has worked on a recent project that required telephone contacts knows that a high proportion of all phones are now answered by machines. The choice you face is whether to leave a message or to call back later in hopes of reaching a person. When you are contacting participants who already know you or your organization, leaving a message on an answering machine may work. Even so, the preferred procedure is to call back two or three times before you leave a message. With "cold calls," where the participant will have no idea who you are, you may want to increase this to five or six attempts at making a personal contact. Of course, keeping track of how often someone has been called requires well-organized recruitment procedures.

If you do leave messages, how can you motivate people to call back? If you have some form of sponsorship or prior contact that will probably motivate the participants, then by all means mention that as your reason for calling. Anything that makes a message seem more personal will help. If you describe the group that you hope they will participate in, have a script that will make it sound interesting to the kinds of people you are calling. It also helps to convey a sense that you are flexible and easy to work with. Give them reasonable options for calling you back, and let them know that there are several possible times when they might fit into a group. If you will be paying people to participate, it helps to mention this fact, but leave information about the exact amount you are offering only when you are certain that it is enough to create an incentive to call you back.

Dealing With Answering Machines

Screening Finds Special Categories of Participants

As we described in Chapter 6, "Deciding on the Group Composition," many focus group projects call for specialized recruiting that assigns specific categories of participants to specific groups. In some cases, you want to ensure that the participants are all relatively homogeneous so that they will have a free-flowing group dynamic. In other cases, you want to use segmentation to compare different categories of participants in different groups. Either way, you will need to screen the participants so that you have the right people in each group.

Chapter 6 summarized several common factors that are used to determine the composition of focus groups, including the following:

- Demographic characteristics
- Experiences
- Attitudes and opinions

These criteria will now serve as screening criteria in recruitment. During an initial contact call, you ask questions that determine whether the potential participant meets your screening criteria and is thus eligible for the group. For example, you might be searching specifically for just one particular kind of participant, or you might be screening lower-income participants in one group and upper-income participants in another. (See "City Government Priorities," a screening script at the end of this chapter, for an example of how to screen for particular characteristics.)

Moderating Focus Groups Discusses How to Deal With "Experts"

The basic purpose of screening is to make sure that you hear from your targeted categories of participants, but screening can also help you eliminate unwanted types of participants. For example, experts, either self-appointed or real, can greatly complicate a moderator's task, so screening questions can help create groups of participants who have similar levels of experience with the topic. Screening can also avoid "focus groupies" by limiting the participants to those who have not been in a focus group recently—typically within the past 6 months.

Screening also generates data. Indeed, most screening forms are based on questionnaires. So, if you are using screening questions, you will want to set up your procedures to capture basic information about each participant, such as demographics. These data can be quite useful during analysis, since they can point to factors that are associated with different points of view. In addition, collecting demographic data during recruitment contacts can let you know something about those who fail to show up for the actual focus group: Are there some categories of participants that you need to work with more closely during recruitment in order to get them to the group itself?

When setting up a screener questionnaire, the goal is to ask the minimum number of questions necessary to determine whether someone is eligible. By ordering the questions to eliminate ineligibles as quickly as possible, you will minimize the time that recruiters spend with people who don't fit your criteria. For instance, if you are looking for low-income, single mothers with children in elementary school, start by asking whether there are any children aged 6 to 12 living in the house, since this will eliminate more people than asking about marital status. In addition, you should wait to ask about more sensitive items, such as income, until after the person has already replied to several of your other requests for information.

Consider the Order of Screening Questions

Although screening is often essential to finding the right categories of participants, it can also greatly complicate your recruitment efforts. The most common problem occurs when the eligibility criteria are so tightly defined that it becomes difficult to locate participants. This will increase the cost of the recruitment effort and may force you to reschedule groups because you have not located enough participants within the original timeline. If you need to ask several questions to locate eligible participants, this can be a sign that you are being overly narrow in your recruitment criteria, since each question will reduce the number of people available. Even when you have only one or two screening criteria, an overly narrow definition of eligibility can turn a small recruitment pool into a rare population.

If overly narrow screening requirements are a concern, monitor your success rates during the first few days of recruitment to examine how many potential participants are being screened out at each step in your screening questionnaire. This will help you locate the specific screening criteria that you should consider "loosening" to increase the size of the recruitment pool. It helps to begin by determining a wider range of participants who will be acceptable if you are indeed unable to locate enough people who meet the more restrictive criteria. In other words, define your "fall-back position" at the start of the recruitment process. This allows you to set up the screening questionnaire so that it first determines who is eligible within the broader range and then asks whether potential participants also meet the narrower criteria. If the narrower criteria prove to be too restrictive, you can recontact the participants who have already met the broader the criteria.

Giving and Receiving Information

When people do agree to participate in a focus group, your further contacts with them will involve both giving and receiving information. On the receiving end, you want, at a minimum, to confirm participants' addresses and phone numbers. This information will be vital for recontacting them during the later stages of recruitment, but it may also be important for contacts that continue beyond the focus groups themselves. For instance, you may need to maintain contact to collect follow-up information, send thank-you notes or summary reports, recruit them for future focus groups, and so on.

Be Sure You Have Accurate Recontact Information

Your contact conversations with future participants also involve giving out information. In almost all cases, you will tell them about the following:

- The subject of your research
- Who will be at the group
- What you need from them as participants
- What you will offer in terms of incentives, refreshments, and so forth
- What kinds of future contacts you will have with them prior to the focus group

How much should you tell the participants about the topic of the research? Inevitably, they will be wondering "what you want," so you do need to give them some basic information about the topic of the group. The basic rule is that you do not want to tell them so much that you "overscript" them, but you also want to avoid telling them so little that you leave them guessing in the dark.

The usual approach is to give a very broad or generic description of the research topic. For example, you may tell participants that you are interested in their "experiences and feelings about . . . ." Focus groups on political topics often tell participants that they will be discussing "the issues that you think are important to your community." Understandably, participants will often push recruiters for more information about the topic of the discussion. In that case, the standard reply is that the recruiters do not have more information, since it is important that "everyone who attends the group starts from the same place." Often, the recruitment team knows very little about the actual content of the focus groups, so it is crucial that they not offer speculations that will mislead participants.

Screening questionnaires also require care, since asking for information not only generates data for you but may also alert participants to your interests. Worse still, it can lead them to assume that you are more interested in something than you really are, based on the fact that you asked about certain topics when you first contacted them. Sometimes, you have questions that you would like to ask, but you are afraid of steering the participants into inappropriate assumptions about the topics for the groups. In that case, consider collecting this information through a questionnaire that participants complete upon arrival at the group, rather than during the recruitment contact. That way, any mistaken assumptions can be cleared up immediately.

Think About the Information Conveyed by Screening Questions

What If You Do Want People to Prepare Before the Group?

For some projects, you want the participants to think about the topic before they begin the discussion. For instance, if you have a lot of material to cover, it will help if participants are well prepared and have a solid understanding of what you want them to talk about. The most common way to handle this is during the time between when participants arrive for the group and when the actual discussion starts. Thus, when participants arrive, they may be given brief questionnaires, often with open-ended items, to stimulate their thinking on the topic.

For some projects, however, there may not be enough time for these activities, or you may need the participants to engage in more preparation than can be accomplished in the 15 minutes or so prior to the group discussion. In addition, there are some categories of participants, such as high-level executives, who may be unwilling to participate unless you provide sufficient detail about the subject of the research. In those cases, there are several available options.

- *Mail out an information sheet as part of the follow-up materials. Rather than trying to discuss the topic over the telephone, assure all participants that they will receive a description in the material that you mail them. This way, everyone will receive a consistent amount of information, so that they all "start from the same place."*

- *Mail out a questionnaire for the participants to bring with them to the group. This will not only provide you with additional information about all participants but will also channel their thinking along the lines that interest you. Often, these questionnaires end with a request to write an open-ended response to a question that will start the group discussion itself.*

- *Give each participant a brief assignment. Usually, this should be something that can be conveyed quickly and clearly during the initial telephone contact and then be reinforced in a subsequent contact or by mail. For example, you might instruct the participants: "Come prepared to talk about the last time that you . . . ." or "Be ready to tell us about two people you know who . . ."*

- *Diaries and logs of experiences represent a more demanding kind of "pre-group assignment." Diaries are especially useful when you want to know exactly how much contact the participants have with a phenomenon. They are also an effective tool for raising people's awareness of taken-for-granted aspects of daily life, by asking them to note and record these things. For example, a study of mosquito control had participants keep a log of their outdoor activities and whether or not they encountered mosquitoes. The advantages of diaries have to be weighed against the additional effort that goes into keeping them and the risk that participants will drop out of the project rather than do this much work. Consequently, projects that combine diary keeping and focus groups nearly always offer substantial monetary incentives.*

In all of these cases, any requests that participants engage in preparation prior to the group will require additional follow-up efforts by the recruitment team. This typically involves scheduling an additional telephone recontact to remind the participant of the preparation that you are requesting.

Another issue about giving out information during recruitment contacts concerns participants' desire to know who the sponsor of the research is. In some cases, the name of the sponsor will be an important part of your recruiting pitch, because it provides a relationship that will encourage people to participate. In other cases, withholding the name of the sponsor may help you get more honest responses from the participants. For example, focus groups that involve commercial products seldom tell the participants which manufacturer's product they will be discussing, and the same is true for work with political campaigns. Withholding the name of the project's sponsor is much less common when the sponsor is a government or nonprofit agency.

When you do not wish to give out the sponsor's name during the recruitment contact, the usual approach is, once again, to offer very general information. Often, it will be enough to identify a larger unit of the sponsoring organization, rather than a specific program. Sometimes, you can compromise by assuring the participants that they will learn who the sponsor is at the end of the group but explaining that you want them to start without any prior assumptions.

A final piece of information that the participant usually receives during the recruitment contact is a sense of who else will be at the focus group. Typically, this can be answered with some variation on "other people like yourself." Where you are using screening criteria to ensure the homogeneity of the members in each group, it is wise to let the participants know that they are being specifically selected to talk with others who share these characteristics. This usually makes the participants feel more confident that they will be talking to others who share their perspectives. In addition, it will minimize the suspicion that may arise when the participants discover the segmentation after they arrive at the group. For example, suppose you tell the participants that you have selected them because you want to find out how they feel about some highly generic topic; when they arrive at the group, they discover that—lo and behold!—everyone there is an

African American male. It would be better to tell them in the beginning that "We are especially interested in hearing the opinions of men from the African American community, so we are setting up a group just for black men such as yourself." In addition, if you are recruiting from a list that supposedly is limited to people who meet your screening criteria, a statement such as the one above provides a good opportunity to ensure that the participant does meet your criteria.

Incentives Encourage Participation

Are incentives really necessary? For the participants, focus groups can be demanding, in terms of their time and travel. For the project sponsors, groups that fail to draw enough participants are expensive—at a minimum, all of the recruitment effort that went into the group was wasted, and it may still be necessary to cover the expenses associated with the moderator, the room rental, and refreshments. So, the cost of incentives often amounts to "cheap insurance," given the higher costs of canceling groups.

When people raise concerns about offering incentives in focus groups, they are almost always thinking in terms of payments in cash, but not all incentives involve money. Although the term *incentive* has become almost a synonym for money in focus group circles, offering incentives really means finding ways to motivate people to participate. Ask yourself, What matters to the participants? In many cases, there are other motivators that are at least as powerful as money. In other cases, offering money may actually offend the participants, such as when they have a strong personal commitment to a charitable organization.

For some topics, the potential participants' personal motivations may provide a sufficient incentive. People are often willing to participate for free when they feel that they will be helping an organization or cause that matters to them. This is especially true when the project will have meaningful outcomes; giving individuals a voice in decisions that matter to them can be a rare gift. The opportunity to share ideas and experiences with peers can also be a powerful motivator. For example, even though pharmaceutical companies routinely pay doctors more than $100 to discuss their prescribing practices, I have had good luck in getting physicians to participate for free in groups that are close to their shared interests, such as handling medical malpractice problems or dealing with difficult diagnostic decisions. So, money may talk, but it is hardly the only motivator that makes people listen.

Even if you do need to offer some tangible inducement to get people to participate, this does not have to be money. In some cases, nonmonetary incentives are more affordable than their cash value. Refreshments or a meal are common alternatives to cash. When you are holding a focus group at a hotel or other conference setting, there frequently will be a considerable savings for using in-house catering services along with a room rental. On more than one occasion, I've found that the kind of catered meal a facility can provide for $15 per person far outshines what you would get for this amount in its dining room or restaurant. Gifts or gift certificates are another kind of nonmonetary incentive that can result in considerable savings. For example, you may be able to locate an organization that will provide gift certificates as a charitable donation. Even if the tax write-off is not available, it may still be possible to solicit donated gifts or gift certificates, since this can be a good form of advertising for the donor. For one set of groups, a bookstore volunteered to give an even larger gift certificate than we requested, after reminding us that it was really a wholesale cost for the store.

Consider Nonmonetary Incentives

If you can't offer cash incentives, how can you develop the kinds of personal motivators or nonmonetary incentives that will aid your recruitment effort? Once again, knowing what matters to the participants is the key, so find informants who can help with decisions about incentives.

Despite these alternatives, money still remains the most powerful form of incentive in focus group recruitment, for any number of reasons. One of the foremost appeals of money is its convenience: You don't have to take it somewhere to trade it in, nor is there any problem in carrying it home. Money not only appeals to everyone, but it also has the same value to all; for example, receiving a nice meal isn't an incentive to someone who doesn't like to eat out. Paying people also levels out the reasons for participating; when there is a fee involved, your participants are not limited just to those who have a special interest in the topic or those who enjoy groups. Finally, in our society, paying people shows respect for what they are doing for you and the time that they are giving you.

A different reason for paying people is that this is the dominant tradition in many types of focus groups. For instance, it would be almost unthinkable not to pay people for attending groups to discuss consumer products. The emphasis on monetary payments in consumer research is reflected in the number of terms its practitioners use to refer to cash incentives; these include *coop fees, honorariums,* and *stipends.*

If you are going to pay people to participate, how much should you offer? We provided some estimates of incentive costs when discussing budgets in Chapter 4. The fundamental rule is that cash costs go up for participants who are more difficult either to locate or to schedule. Members of the general public may be available for $25 to $35, while professionals and executives may require amounts well over $100. If you are trying to recruit rare categories of participants, you may save money on your total recruitment costs by offering a higher incentive. Imagine that it takes your recruiter 2 hours of calling just to locate a potential participant; if you don't offer a sufficient incentive to convince that person, then it is going to cost you another 2 hours of recruiting to find another one.

This last point is more general: By speeding up recruitment, incentives can help you trade off time for money. Often, the monetary cost of offering incentives is well worth the time that you would otherwise spend on a protracted, low-budget recruitment process.

KEY POINT

Incentives Pose a Trade-Off Between Time and Money

Timing and Location Make a Difference

Another important element in successful recruitment is picking times and locations that will be convenient for your participants. This requires an understanding of what makes a difference to them. What are their schedules like? What aspects of a location will make it either easier or harder for them?

The most common way to think about when to schedule a focus group is to pick a time that is likely to be convenient for both the participants and the research team. The blocks of time that usually meet these criteria are late afternoon and early evening, roughly from 5:00 to 7:00 and 7:00 to 9:00 (or 7:30 to 9:30, if you are going to schedule a pair of groups back to back). Allowing for the half hour of driving time that it may take to get to the groups, the first of these time slots basically requires someone to leave work or home at 4:30 and not be back until 7:30, so it includes the dinner hour. The later time slot essentially asks someone to be done with dinner by 6:30 or 7:00 to depart for the group, with a promise of returning home by 9:30 or 10:00.

Behind these common time slots is some straightforward reasoning about what else might conflict with the focus group. Work and family life are the most obvious issues. When you are working with participants from the general population, these will be the basic concerns. If you are working with people who have especially demanding work and family schedules, then you will have to give special attention to their availability. For example, busy executives may be more willing to squeeze in a morning meeting. Similarly, you might try scheduling a mothers' group at a day care center during the time they would ordinarily be picking up their children (under the assumption that you would bear any cost for the additional hour or two of childcare). In contrast, when you are working with participants who have fewer constraints with regard to either their work life or their family life, then you can be more flexible in your scheduling.

Along with picking a time during the day goes a concern about which days to use. For obvious reasons, Mondays through Thursdays are most commonly paired with the 5:00 to 7:00 and 7:00 to 9:00 time slots. Saturday groups are unusual, as it takes a strong incentive for people to schedule something into what is usually their longest block of free time. Besides the day of the week, you also have to consider possible conflicts with special events and holidays. Anyone who has ever scheduled an evening group when a local sports team is in the playoffs knows the importance of special events. Among holidays, it is almost lore that one should not try to schedule focus groups from the end of November until the beginning of January. Still, for any aspect of scheduling, the real issue is what matters to your participants. Our schedule on one project forced us to hold groups in the week before Christmas, but we were offering $50 incentives to recruit groups of low-income recipients, so we had no trouble recruiting people.

Offer Multiple Times During Recruitment Contacts

If possible, it helps to schedule all of the times for a set of focus groups before you begin making your recruitment contacts. That way, when you contact a potential participant, you can offer a choice of dates and times. Otherwise, recruiting for a single group forces you to locate people whose schedules correspond to that one time slot.

When choosing locations, the basic rule is the same as with selecting the time for the group: Think about what will matter to the participants. Convenience is often the dominant concern. In terms of the geographical location, ask yourself, Where will they be coming from, and where will they be going afterwards? Will they all be driving, or will they be using public transportation? Remember, too, that convenience is not just driving distance, because some places are more difficult to get to than others, and parking can be a major hassle at some locations.

Psychological factors are also important in selecting locations. Does this place have "meaning" for the participants? Sometimes, issues of meaning run counter to issues of convenience. For example, when the project involves a location that the participants often visit, such as a work site or a school, it is tempting to hold the groups there to maximize convenience. Psychologically, however, it might be better to use a more neutral setting, especially when you want the participants to offer new ideas or otherwise move away from their routine thinking.

Sometimes, you are working with groups that have obvious special needs:

- *Those with physical disabilities may need a location that meets the accessibility criteria spelled out in the Americans with Disabilities Act.*

- *Parents may need to have childcare available.*

- *People with limited transportation options may need a van shuttle, taxi service, or assistance with public transportation.*

When your entire group consists of such participants, their needs are obvious, but you should not ignore these issues just because you are running a "general population" group. The reality is that someone in nearly every group will have "special needs." So, think through your assumptions to make sure that the locations and facilities you are providing will meet the needs of all of your potential participants. At a minimum, if you know your situation may create problems for some types of participants, let people know that during the recruitment contacts; this may save both you and participants the frustration of having them show up for a group where you cannot accommodate them.

TIP

**Consider
Special Needs**

Plan Ahead to Minimize No-Show Rates

One of the most common problems that beginners have in focus groups is the failure of scheduled participants to show up. Too often, you are confronted with the question of whether you should go ahead with a group of only three or four participants when you had planned for eight or even ten. Sometimes, your group simply will not work with too few participants. Sometimes, if you were expecting to hear about a range of experiences from a number of people to get a lively discussion started, your questions will not work with just a few people. Other times, the smaller group of two to four participants can yield valuable information.

A high no-show rate raises questions about data quality. Can you really believe that those who did show up have the same opinions and experiences as those who did not? A high no-show rate may point to a biased sample, due to unknown issues about willingness to participate. In many respects, no-show rates in focus groups are like nonresponse rates in surveys, because they indicate that something was wrong with the basic procedures for bringing people into the study. A high no-show rate may thus cast doubts on the merits of the data.

KEY POINT

**High No-Show
Rates Raise
Questions About
Data Quality**

One solution to the problem of no-shows is to "over-recruit," that is, to invite more participants than you really need so you can be sure that you will have enough. One way to think about over-recruiting is that it is like insurance, because it can save you the cost of a group that would otherwise either produce limited data or have to be canceled altogether. As a general rule, over-recruiting by one or two people is OK and may well be a wise allowance for the complications that arise in people's schedules. If you find that you need to over-recruit beyond this minimal level in order to have enough participants who actually show up, then you need to revise your recruitment procedures.

There are several reasons why extensive over-recruiting is not a very good solution, however. First, it can be expensive, not only in terms of incentives but also in terms of the extra recruitment effort that it takes to schedule additional people. Second, it can be inconvenient if too many people actually show up, although there are usually ways to handle this situation. Finally, over-recruiting does not handle the problem of bias due to the differences between those who do show up and those who do not; it merely guarantees that you will find enough of the former.

There are, however, some cases when it does make sense to consider over-recruiting. For instance, if the staff you are using does not have much experience recruiting for focus groups, they may schedule people who say they will come but are not really serious about attending. The same thing can happen when you are working with a new category of potential participants that you have never tried to recruit before, even if your recruitment procedures have worked well elsewhere. Still, these are special cases. If you are going to do focus groups on a regular basis, then you need to develop recruitment procedures that use minimal levels of over-recruiting.

The first step to reducing the no-show rate is to consider this basic question: Why do people fail to show up? Aside from the scheduling problems that may eliminate one or two people, high no-show rates are often due to what social psychologists call "diffusion of responsibility." Diffusion of responsibility occurs in group settings because each individual can easily conclude that the other members of the group will take care of whatever needs to be done. So, if your potential participants get an offer to do something other than your focus group, they may well conclude that "everyone else" will show up and it doesn't matter if they skip the group. In other words, it is easy for group members to conclude that their participation is not all that important because

Moderating Focus Groups Discusses What to Do With Too Many Participants

the rest of the group is there to handle the problem. Understanding this line of thinking points the way to the fundamental solution to high no-show rates: Your recruitment procedures need to convince everyone you schedule that participating is important.

Minimizing no-show rates starts with the first contact. Your contact script should convey to participants that their contribution is important and that an agreement to participate is a commitment on their part. Too often, novice recruiters concentrate on the goal of getting enough people to say "Yes," without listening to hear whether the person either agrees that the group is important or is truly willing to make a commitment to attend. Don't oversell the groups. Realize that sometimes the easiest way for a potential participant to deal with a "demon recruiter" is just to say "Yes," because there doesn't seem to be any other way to get the recruiter to go away. If potential participants do sound uncertain, ask them to be "alternates," and tell them you will call back in a couple of days; by then, they will have decided one way or the other.

Once you have an initial agreement to participate, your recruitment efforts shift to follow-up contacts. One of the simplest reasons that projects have high no-show rates is that they fail to maintain enough contact with the participants. Getting someone to say "Yes" during an initial telephone contact is a good start, but you need to follow up. Follow-up contacts give you an opportunity to maintain the participants' interest in the groups. They also let you convey how important it is that the participants make good on their commitment to attend.

The most basic kind of follow-up contact is a confirmation letter. As soon as possible after the initial agreement to participate in a focus group, mail a letter that thanks participants for being part of your project; reminds them of the date, time, and location of the group; and includes any additional information, such as maps or a preliminary questionnaire. More than just information, the confirmation letter also needs to convey a sense that their ideas and experiences matter to you—that participating is important.

A confirmation letter should be as personal as possible. Small things like hand addressing a letter and using a real stamp signal your interest in the person you are writing to. Similarly, it also helps to use an official envelope and letterhead stationery.

KEY POINT

Emphasize That Participating Is Important

TIP

Ask People Who Are Uncertain to Be "Alternates"

KEY POINT

Follow-Up Contacts Are Essential

EXAMPLE

**A Confirmation
Letter**

[Date]

[Participant's name and address]

Thank you for agreeing to participate in the focus group that the Institute on Aging at Portland State University is holding on July 21st at 5:00 at the Valley Inn. Enclosed with this letter is a map and directions that show you how to get to the Valley Inn. We will be meeting in their conference room, and the staff at the front desk will be happy to show you where that room is.

As we explained in our earlier telephone call, the purpose of this group is to hear about your retirement plans. You will be part of a group of seven or eight people from the local area who are all either recently retired or considering retiring soon. We know that people have a great many different ideas about what they might do when they retire, and we are very interested in hearing your thoughts on this subject.

The session will begin at 5:00 and will end at 7:00. We know how valuable your time is, and we will respect everyone's schedules by both starting and ending on time. So, please allow yourself enough time to reach the Valley Inn by 5:00; if you arrive after the discussion has started, we may not be able to include you.

We will provide a light buffet supper and pay you $25.00 for your participation. As we told you in our telephone conversation, we will be tape recording your discussion so that we can keep a careful record of the things that we hear from you and the others. We will, as we promised, take every step to maintain your privacy.

Once again, we are glad you have accepted our invitation to participate in this group. Of course, the success of any group depends on each of its members, so we are counting on you. If you cannot attend for any reason, please call us at (503) 555-5555 as soon as possible.

We look forward to meeting with you on July 21st.

Sincerely yours,

David L. Morgan
Project Coordinator

The second basic follow-up contact is a reminder telephone call right before the group, typically the night before. This may jog the memory of some participants, or it may give you an early alert to no-shows (possibly allowing you to contact any alternate participants that you have).

Whenever your recruitment procedures differ from the standard approach of contacting and scheduling participants for a focus group within the next two weeks, you will need to adapt your follow-up procedures accordingly. If there is a longer time between the initial contact and the group, you may want to send a reminder postcard that will arrive a week or so before the group, in addition to the immediate confirmation letter and the reminder call right before. If you are recruiting participants through an existing meeting or conference, you will want to have contact with them once they arrive on-site—possibly by leaving a message at their hotel room. Whatever your specific recruitment circumstances are, you need to build in a follow-up strategy that minimizes no-show rates by keeping participants mindful of their important commitment to be there at your focus group.

Professional Recruiting Services Are an Option

Most large cities have commercial firms that will recruit participants for focus groups. Typically, these businesses offer a range of services. They may have their own lists of potential participants from past projects, or they may already be set up to do random digit dialing recruitment. These firms usually specialize in making telephone contacts, using a well-trained staff and a room full of equipment. They can work with you to iron out the details of recruitment scripts and confirmation letters so that you effectively communicate your message to potential participants. They also have widespread experience with screening to help you locate specific categories of participants. When time is of the essence, they may be able to add staff to get things done quickly. Finally, they can provide very accurate estimates about no-show rates, so there is little worry that a group will have to be canceled.

Of course, all this comes at a cost. If you are working with participants from the general population, the recruitment firm may charge $50 per person or more for each participant who shows up at the focus group. This is based on the assumption that you are paying each participant an incentive of $35 to $50. The total cost per participant can thus be close to $100; there is, however, considerable variation from place to place, with costs generally being lower in smaller cities.

It is important to understand that these costs are actually based on the staff time that it takes to locate your participants. Anything that makes it harder to locate people or to get them to say "Yes" will thus drive up the costs. In particular, lowering the dollar value of incentives may not really cut costs, because it will increase the staff time involved in recruitment. Fortunately, one of the advantages of working with professional recruitment firms is their prior experience, and they should be able to give you good advice about what it will take to motivate participants.

The price of recruitment goes up once you step beyond the general population. If you want a more specialized sample or a more difficult-to-reach group, this will either take more staff time or require the use of limited-access recruiting sources. For groups that involve professionals or executives, the costs can easily reach $200 to $300 per participant. These estimates are based on an incentive that amounts to about half of the total cost, so the total cost would really be $300 to $500.

Whose List?

As we noted in the first section of this chapter, many recruitment firms have lists of participants from prior focus groups. Working with these lists can save you time, because you are dealing with willing participants. In fact, this may be the one situation where being able to leave messages on answering machines is actually helpful! Because the recruitment firm's costs are typically based on staff time, saving time also amounts to saving money.

Still, you should be wary of using participants who were originally recruited for other purposes. Does the recruitment firm have information on the topics for the previous groups that each person has participated in? Do they know how many groups each person has participated in, and when the most recent one was? High-quality firms keep databases that allow them to answer such questions, and to screen out people if they have been in groups too recently or have discussed topics that conflict with yours.

What if you have your own list? Most professional recruitment firms are willing to work with existing lists. You will, however, have to confirm this on a case-by-case basis. Sometimes, these firms may raise issues about using your list, based on their past experience, and they may raise concerns that you had not even thought about.

Suppose you are considering a professional recruitment firm; how do you pick one? The first step should be to use your networks: Get advice from people you trust and who will understand your needs. Do the people you know have relevant experiences with recruitment firms, or can they refer you to someone who does? If you can't start from personal contacts, the Yellow Pages and marketing research directories are good sources for likely candidates. Nearly all recruitment firms have client lists of people they have worked with in the past, and contacting these people is a good way to get realistic expectations about what a recruiting firm can and cannot do, what it will really cost, and so forth. If you do make inquiries, do so in a professional manner: Check with the people at the recruitment firm about the most appropriate ways to approach any of their past clients, and when you do talk to these people, treat them as sources of factual information, not as inside tipsters.

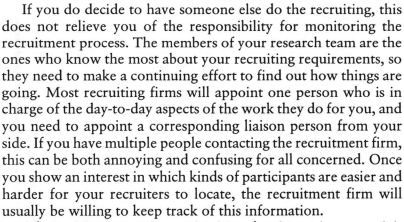

The biggest benefit of using a recruitment firm occurs when a project involves a lot of telephone calling. Recruitment firms are set up to handle precisely this sort of work. The next biggest benefit of recruitment firms is their experience and expertise. If you are planning to do focus groups on a regular basis, you may well want to go to the effort that it takes to create for yourself the facilities and expertise that already exist in professional recruitment firms. Otherwise, you may be wise to take advantage of the services that these firms are designed to offer.

Before you decide to go with a recruitment firm, however, there is one further consideration. How well will their staff represent you in contacts with potential participants? Where you have an ongoing relationship with these participants, this can be a special concern. It is also an issue when you are dealing with groups that may be a "tough sell." In some cases, you might have more success through using the seasoned skills of a professional recruiter. In other cases, your own staff may have a much better sense of how to approach categories of participants that they work with on a routine basis. This comes down to a question of the kinds of experience and expertise that will be most valuable for assisting your specific recruitment efforts.

BACKGROUND

When to Use a Recruitment Firm

If you do decide to have someone else do the recruiting, this does not relieve you of the responsibility for monitoring the recruitment process. The members of your research team are the ones who know the most about your recruiting requirements, so they need to make a continuing effort to find out how things are going. Most recruiting firms will appoint one person who is in charge of the day-to-day aspects of the work they do for you, and you need to appoint a corresponding liaison person from your side. If you have multiple people contacting the recruitment firm, this can be both annoying and confusing for all concerned. Once you show an interest in which kinds of participants are easier and harder for your recruiters to locate, the recruitment firm will usually be willing to keep track of this information.

The main concerns in monitoring others' recruitment activities are making sure that you get the right people and that you are aware of any factors that influence who is or is not in the groups. This can be crucial in ensuring the quality of your data. For example, it may well be that the only way to meet your time and cost requirements is to broaden the recruitment strategy to include a wider range of participants; you need to know this in order to make sure that your conclusions take into account the sample of participants you actually heard from.

KEY POINT

It Is Your Responsibility to Monitor Recruitment Procedures

Checklist for Successful Recruitment

Overall, regardless of whether you are doing your own recruiting or hiring someone to do it for you, you need to consider a series of basic issues.

CHECKLIST

**Successful
Recruitment**

Convey a sense that the research will be interesting and worthwhile.

Start by thinking about why someone would want to participate in this project. This isn't just about your desire to get information from them—there has to be a reason why the focus group will be rewarding to the people you are trying to recruit. Whenever you contact them, you need to communicate that what they are doing is important and interesting.

Make the contacts personal. Recruitment is not a mechanical exercise.

It is the beginning of the person-to-person interaction that is at the heart of focus groups. So, whether your contact is in person, on the telephone, or by letter, make sure that you are connecting with the potential participants in a way that will be meaningful to them.

Build on existing relationships whenever possible.

"Cold calls" take the most effort. If you can build on an existing organization membership or other tie, you are more likely to find people who will not just listen to your recruitment pitch but actually say "Yes."

Use appropriate screening criteria.

Make sure that the participants are the ones that you need. When a group has even one or two "mismatched" participants, it can greatly affect the dynamics of that discussion. At the same time, do not make your screening criteria so restrictive that it is difficult to find participants.

Offer incentives.

The purpose of incentives is to increase motivation. Motivated participants are easier to recruit and more likely to attend. So, any incentives that increase their motivation will make your job easier. To create incentives, think about what will motivate participants; money may be the most straightforward incentive, but there are many other sources of motivation.

Make participation as convenient as possible.

Choose a time and place that will meet the participants' needs. Think about any issues that may conflict with attending your group, so you can make appropriate arrangements for refreshments, parking, childcare, and so on.

Follow up.

Recruitment is more than getting someone to say "Yes." The real job does not end until the participants actually attend the groups. By sending additional materials and making confirmation calls, you let them know that you expect them to follow through on their initial commitment.

At every stage, let them know that their participation is important.

> Getting someone to attend a focus group is usually more important to you than it is to them! The success of your research is riding on the recruitment process, but for the participants, it may just be one more thing to squeeze into their calendars. The obvious solution is to convince them that being in this group is a high priority. The more important the group is to them, the more likely you are to recruit a set of motivated and committed participants.

Examples of Recruitment Scripts

African Americans and Healthy Eating Habits

Background

These groups were conducted to follow up on a yearlong medical research project that involved changing the nutrition habits and eating patterns of African Americans. It had been difficult to sign people up for that original project, and now the same research team was about to undertake a new set of projects on the same topic. The goal in the focus groups was to learn more about how to get members of the African American community to take part in this kind of project.

In essence, this was a "post-program evaluation" to learn about how people had reacted to aspects of the prior project before undertaking a new one.

The recruitment contacts were based on a list of those who had been in the earlier project. This would be similar to other projects where you are contacting people who have some prior experience with your group or organization. Note that because of this prior contact, we were more willing to leave answering machine messages and to explain the purpose of our call to other members of the participant's household if the participant was not at home.

The script assumes that the recruitment would be done by relatively untrained staff members at each of several different locations. To ensure consistency in how the volunteers used the script, we included relatively explicit directions. The script also includes a list of frequently asked questions (parallel with the recruiting script itself), so that the recruiters would be prepared to respond to the potential participants' concerns.

Screening Script

1. Contacting the potential participant

   Hello, may I please speak to [name]?

   If the person is not at home:

   When would be a good time to reach [him/her]?

   If the person has moved, try to get a new phone number.

2. Explaining the project

   My name is [your full name], and I'm calling from [name of your center].

   You were in our project on Healthy Eating Habits. Now we're holding a focus group to follow up on that project, and I want to offer you the chance to be in that. This is a group interview that would last about 2 hours, and we would pay you $[amount].

   You would get together with other people who were in the Healthy Eating Habits project to have a discussion and answer some questions for us. There would just be this one meeting.

   Can I tell you a little more about this?

   First of all, the session that we're trying to set up is on [day] at [time]. Is that something that could fit into your schedule?

   If the participant is not available, thank the person and end the call.

   If the participant is available, continue with:

   We want to find out more about why some people are willing to be in projects like that study on Healthy Eating Habits, while others are less willing. Right now, we're trying to put together a group of people who were all in the Healthy Eating Habits project so we can hear your thoughts.

   We're especially interested in finding out what people in the African American community think about projects like ours. We hope to do more projects on how African Americans can have more healthy eating habits. So, we need to learn how people in the African American community feel about participating in projects such as this.

But all that is in the future. Right now, this focus group will only happen once and it will last just 2 hours. We won't try to sell you anything, and we won't try to sign you up for anything else. Does this sound like it would work for you?

3. Scheduling the session

The session would be at [location] and, again, it would be on [date]. We would start at [time] and end by [time]. If I do put your name down, it's very important that we have everyone show up. Do you think you can come?

It's also very important that you be there by [start time]; will you have any problem getting there on time?

Again, we'll be paying you $[amount]. The way we will handle that is [describe your local payment procedures].

We'll also be serving [describe food or refreshments].

The group itself will consist of six or seven other people, all from the African American community, who, like yourself, were in the Healthy Eating Habits project. Most of the time that you are there, you'll be talking among yourselves in a group discussion.

We will be tape recording that session so that we have a good sense of what people said. We will keep that tape, and anything you say, completely confidential. We don't expect anybody to be saying anything too threatening, but even so, our first priority is to protect your privacy.

Also, I want to emphasize that once you come to this session, anything you do there will be completely voluntary, and you'll be free to leave at any time for any reason.

I'd like to mail you a letter confirming your participation in this focus group, along with a map and a reminder of the date and time. What is the best address to send that to? [Get mailing address.]

I also need to let you know that we will be starting right on time at [time] on [date]. So, if you get to the session after the discussion has started, we may not be able to include you, and we may not be able to pay you either. So, it is very important that you try to get there on time.

So everyone remembers, we will be calling you back the evening before the group to remind you about it. Is this the best number to reach you at if we call on [day before group]?

Thank you very much. We'll be looking forward to seeing you on [date].

Frequently Asked Questions

1. Contacting the potential participant

    What if the person I'm trying to reach is not home and I get someone else?

    Find out when would be a good time to reach the potential participant.

    What if the person I am talking to promises to have the potential participant call me back?

    That's OK, but it is best for you to reach the potential participant directly. Make a note of when you called and then, if you have not heard from the person within 2 days, call back at a different time of day.

    What if the person who answers wants to know who I am and why I'm calling?

    Go ahead and give your name and the name of your center. Tell the person you are talking to:

    "We want to offer [him/her] the chance to be in a focus group. That would be a group discussion that would last about 2 hours and pays $[amount]. This would just be a one-time session, and it would not involve any medical tests or procedures. We're trying to bring together a group of people to tell us their opinions about some of the things that we do at [name of center]. What would be a good time to reach [name]?"

    What if I reach an answering machine?

    The first time this happens, make a note of it and call back at a different time. If you still get an answering machine, leave a message like this:

    "My name is [your full name], and I'm calling from [name of your center].

I want to offer you the chance to be in a focus group that we're holding. This is a group interview that would last about 2 hours, and we would pay you $[amount].

This would not involve any medical procedures or tests of any kind. Instead, you would get together with a group of people like yourself to have a discussion and answer some questions for us.

I'd be happy to give you some more information, and I promise not to try to talk you into doing something that doesn't interest you. So, if you would like to find out more about this, please call me [(pause) . . . your name] at [(pause) . . . your phone number]."

2. Explaining the project

What if the participant asks, "Why did you pick me? How did you get my name?"

Tell the person: "We're contacting everyone who was in the Healthy Eating Habits study to find out if you would be willing to come back and tell us more about your experiences."

If the person seems concerned or suspicious, have a name and telephone number for someone higher up in your center to speak to resolve any concerns.

What is a focus group?

Explain: "It is a group interview where we bring seven or eight people together to talk about things that you all have in common. We'll have some questions for you to answer, but mostly you'll be talking with each other."

What if the person is unsure whether to participate?

First, make sure that the time is workable (don't waste your time trying to recruit people who can't fit the group into their schedule).

If they are potentially available, don't pressure them. Tell them that you will call back in a couple of days, if you still have an opening in the group. Offer to give your name and telephone number.

If you do call people back who were reluctant the first time, listen carefully to hear how interested or willing they really are. Some people will say "yes" from a sense of obligation when what they really mean is, "maybe, if I find time." Tell them that it is very important that everyone who agrees to come actually shows up. Accept only solid commitments to attend.

What if the person is unsure whether the group will fit into his or her schedule?

Same as above: Offer to call back in a couple of days. For people who sound genuinely interested, you may want to call back more than once. But avoid scheduling people who truly do not know whether or not they can make it. Accept only solid commitments to attend.

3. Scheduling the session

Make sure that all potential participants understand that there is only one time that this group will be held. Make sure they understand that they are making a commitment for a specific day and time.

What if they want to bring someone else along?

Emphasize that they themselves are the ones that we want to have in the group and that only they will be paid.

If another adult does come (e.g., as a source of transportation), he or she will have to wait outside.

What about childcare?

Each center will have to decide what it can and cannot offer. Describe your own local arrangements.

What if they do not want to give out their address?

Emphasize that it is important to mail the information out to everyone. Tell them that you are not connected to any other organization and that you will keep their name and address confidential, just as you will keep everything that they say in the group confidential. Nor will you ever give or sell their name to any other organization or mailing list.

If necessary, have a name and telephone number for someone higher up in your center to phone if they still have concerns.

City Government Priorities

Background

This project brought together residents of a small city to discuss the issues that were of greatest importance to them. It was commissioned by the local city government. The groups were segmented according to whether or not the participants had children in the local school system.

The recruitment was done through a "reverse city directory" that was organized by addresses, and thus allowed us to place telephone numbers of people living throughout all areas within the city. The recruiters were two students taking a course at a local community college. They both had prior experience with telephone sales and recruitment, so this script contains considerably less "supporting material" than the previous example.

Screening Script

Eligibility Requirements

- Over 18 years old
- Has lived in [city] more than 2 years
- Gender balance (no fewer than three men or women in each group)

Introduction

My name is [your full name], and I'm calling from [community college].

We are working on a project to find out more about how people who live here feel about the quality of life in [city].

[If you are looking for a particular gender and the person on phone does not match what you are seeking, ask:]

We want to be sure we talk to both men and women about this, and right now we're looking for more [men/women]. Is there a [man/woman] in your household that I might talk to?

We're going to be bringing together some of the people like you who live in this area for small group discussions to talk about the quality here in [city]. Would you be interested in hearing more about these focus groups?

Screening Questions

We do have a couple of things that we need to check on.

1. What about your age? Are you in your 20s, 30s, 40s . . . ?

    _____ 20s
    _____ 30s
    _____ 40s
    _____ 50s
    _____ 60s
    _____ 70+

    [If the person is too young, explain that we need people who are of voting age and ask if there is anyone over 18 in the household.]

2. How long have you been living in [city]?

    _____ years

    [If less than 2 years, explain that we are particularly interested in changes that people have seen over the past 5 to 10 years, and thank them.]

Scheduling for Eligible Participants

Now, let me tell you more about what we're doing. You'll be getting together with seven or eight of your neighbors and we'll have refreshments.

Two of the teachers from here at [community college] will actually be leading the groups. We'll be talking to you for about an hour and a half, getting you to talk about your experiences and feelings about living in this area.

We will be tape recording the discussion so we don't lose anything, but anything you say will be kept confidential. In other words, we won't use your name in anything we do.

Does this sound like something that would interest you?

[If not, ask, "Can you give me some idea why that is?"]

_____

_____

For those who are interested:

For those who are interested:

OK, let me get a little bit more information about you.

3. About your education, did you finish high school? [If yes, did you finish college?]

_____ Less than high school
_____ High school graduate
_____ Some college (or technical)
_____ Finished college

4. What kind of work do you usually do?

_____

5. Do you currently have any children in the [city] school system?

_____ Yes (Groups 1 & 3)
_____ No   (Groups 2 & 4)

Right now, we are looking for people to attend a discussion on [date/time] at [location]. Would that be a time that you could come talk to us?

[Start with first date that matches their response to question #5. If they cannot make that date, offer the second date.]

Scheduled date: _____

Closing

We will be sending you some information, including a map and some instructions on parking, so I want to confirm that we have the right address. Do you live at . . . ?

I do need to let you know that we will get going right on time at [time] on [date], so please try to be there then. If you do get there after the discussion has already started, we may not be able to include you.

We will call you back to remind you on the day that the group will be meeting. If we call you on [date of group] during the day, would this be a good number to reach you at? [If not, get daytime number or agree to call with reminder the night before.]

If an emergency comes up and you are unable to attend, would you please call [telephone number] and let us know?

Do you have any questions for us?

• Who's paying for this?

Part of the money comes from the city government and part of it comes from [community college]. Most of the people working on this project are volunteers, like me, so we're really trying to keep our costs down.

• What are the questions you're going to ask us?

We'll be asking about your experiences with the various things that are either good or bad about living here. Also, we're interested in your opinions about how things here are changing, either for better or worse.

• Will I hear about the results of this study?

We plan to put this all together into a written report that will be available, and we'll have a public meeting to discuss that report when we present it. That meeting will be in a couple of months, and there will be plenty of announcements about it.

10

Setting Up
the Sessions

Overview

Choosing Locations
Focus Groups in Public Meeting Rooms
Using a Professional Facility
Focus Groups in Private Homes
At Any Location, Consider Food

One unavoidable aspect of planning for focus groups is selecting the location where the discussions will actually occur. Indeed, many of the other choices you make will be contingent on what is or is not possible at the given location. So, although choosing the room where the groups happen may seem like one of the most mundane aspects of focus groups, it can make a fateful difference.

Choosing Locations

Locations for focus groups must meet the needs of both the research team and the participants. From the research team's point of view, the primary concerns are the ability to hold a discussion and capture data:

- Will the participants all be able to see and hear each other?
- Will there be a minimum of distractions and interruptions?
- Will it be straightforward to capture the data, either by observing or recording?

From the participants' point of view, convenience and comfort are the main concerns:

- How easy will it be to reach the facility?
- Is parking available?
- Do the facilities make it pleasant to sit and talk for up to 2 hours?
- Do the facilities convery a pleasant atmosphere without negative feelings?

Chapter 9 Discusses Choosing a Location

There are three basic choices that routinely meet both the research team's and the participants' needs: existing meeting rooms, specially designed professional facilities, and people's homes. This chapter will concentrate on using existing meeting rooms for focus groups, since this is the option that raises the most choices. Compared with setting up a focus group in a meeting room, professional facilities require little additional planning because they are already designed to provide an optimal setting for precisely this purpose. At the other extreme, setting up a focus group in someone's living room requires the researchers to be both polite and creative in adapting to whatever they find. Meeting rooms thus provide neither the certainty of professional facilities nor the irreducible uncertainty of working in private homes. Pick the right conference room and everything will go smoothly. Pick the wrong room and it will be a constant source of hassles that interfere with the session.

Focus Groups In Public Meeting Rooms

The diagram in Figure 10.1 shows several of the characteristics of an ideal focus group setting. The seating arrangements are a central consideration. This diagram shows a rectangular layout, since this is by far the most common option in existing meeting rooms. Professional facilities are somewhat more likely to provide round or oval tables. Although round tables are quite literally legendary for their ability to bring people into face-to-face contact, they are by no means a requirement for focus groups.

The most serious limitation of a rectangular layout is the danger of isolating some participants too far from the moderator.

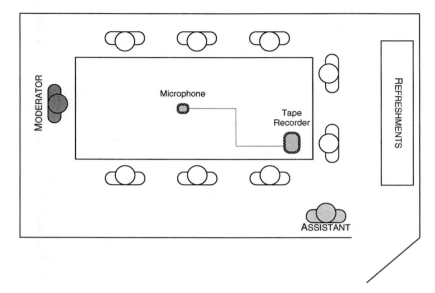

Figure 10.1. Setup for a focus group in a public meeting room.

When you have a choice, avoid long, narrow tables that put too much distance between those who are near the moderator and those at the far end of the table. Long, narrow layouts also place the moderator at the "head of the table." This layout is quite common in boardrooms, making these rooms most suitable for more structured groups, where the goal is to draw attention to the moderator. In contrast, boardrooms and other layouts that involve long tables are more problematic for less structured groups, where the moderator's goal is to facilitate a free-flowing discussion among the participants themselves.

Chapter 5 Discusses Structure in Groups

The diagram highlights another typical feature of the seating arrangements—the placement of the moderator and the assistant. Putting the assistant closer to the door makes it easier to handle any late arrivals or early departures. This arrangement can also minimize disruption to the group by allowing the assistant to talk in the hall to anyone who arrives late or leaves early. In addition, placing the moderator away from the door minimizes the impact of any distractions on his or her attention.

This setup includes an audiotape recorder, placed where the assistant can easily change the tape. Some moderators, however, prefer to have two tape recorders, one at each end of the table. The simple reason for using two recorders is to provide a backup on the data. Using two recorders also doubles the number of electrical outlets that are necessary, however, making it necessary to string more cords and cables around the room. This additional

Moderating Focus Groups **Has More Advice About Setting Up Rooms**

wiring can be a serious problem in a tight room, since it presents a "trip hazard" when people attempt to move around. All things considered, it is definitely preferable to work in a room that offers more options for connecting the recording equipment.

This diagram does not include a video camera, because such elaborate setups are not usually used in this kind of room. If videotaping is necessary, the camera would be placed on a high tripod behind the the moderator and aimed over the moderator's head or shoulder. From this position, a wide-angle lens setting provides a shot of the whole group.

A final feature of this room is a space that is set aside for refreshments, name cards, and so forth. In the diagram, this area is located near the door, so that participants can be greeted here as they arrive. Some moderators prefer to have the participants meet each other socially before the group and not to be seated until the group is ready to start. If there is a foyer or entryway near the door, that layout gives the participants room to mill about prior to the group.

CHECKLIST

Visiting the Room Beforehand

When you have never used a particular room before, it pays to check it out before the first group. Here are some things to consider:

- *Are appropriate tables and chairs already available?*
- *Are there well-placed electrical plugs for recording equipment?*
- *Will noise levels or other distractions be a problem during the group?*
- *Are there windows that will create visual distractions or disrupt videotaping?*
- *If there are refreshments, how will they be served?*
- *How will you handle participants as they arrive, before the group starts?*
- *How will you handle late arrivals, after the group starts?*

Using a Professional Facility

The diagram in Figure 10.2 shows a room in a professional focus group facility. Compared with the previous diagram, some things have been both deleted and added. The most significant deletion is the separate recording equipment. In a professional facility, the recording equipment is built into the room itself. Microphones are typically placed in the ceiling, where they are not only out of the way but positioned to pick up the entire discussion. A video camera may also be mounted in the ceiling; if so, it will be placed

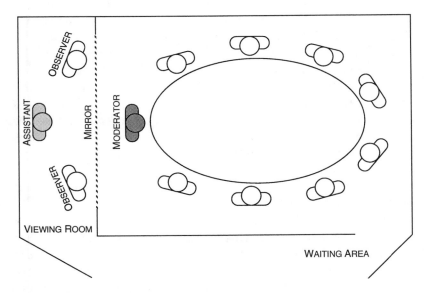

Figure 10.2. Setup for a focus group in a professional facility.

behind the moderator so that it can show the group from the moderator's perspective.

The most significant addition to the room is a viewing area behind a one-way mirror. This area is situated behind the moderator, so the observers can watch the group itself. Some facilities also have the option of closing a set of drapes over the mirror, in case there is a need to assure the participants that they are not being observed. As a general rule, the participants are unaware of either the people behind the mirror or what they are doing.

Where the facility has been built specifically for focus groups, the viewing area may be slightly elevated or arranged in tiers, to improve the sight lines out into the room itself. Viewing areas frequently include some provision for serving refreshments, since the observers may also be spending their dinner hour at the facility. Indeed, some viewing rooms are quite luxurious, allowing for the dubious practice of wining and dining the observers.

The actual recording equipment is usually located within the viewing area, to minimize its potential for distracting the participants. The built-in microphones in the room provide the sound to the observers at a controlled volume level. When a video camera is not present in the focus group room itself, a camera can be positioned behind the mirror. Alternatively, when there is a ceiling-mounted video camera, this can eliminate the need for a one-way mirror, because viewing can occur on TV monitors anywhere within the facility, or even at remote locations.

Figure 10.1 shows the assistant in the viewing room, but the assistant will often move around during the course of the group. While the participants are arriving, this set-up allows the assistant to greet them in the waiting area, where refreshments can also be served. After escorting the participants to the table and seating them, the assistant usually moves to the viewing room, with the observers, and remains there for most of the session. This allows the observers to ask questions, as well as to make requests that the assistant can relay to the moderator. The assistant thus represents a line of communication between the observers and the moderator. For example, the interview guide might have an "open spot" near the end for a question that the assistant could bring in from the observers.

The doors to the focus group room and the viewing area are also worth mentioning. In this diagram, each of these rooms has a separate entry to smooth the assistant's movements between the two areas. From the participants' vantage point, the assistant simply comes and goes through the hall door; they are generally unaware of the assistant's role in communicating with the observers. In some facilities, there is a door that leads directly from the viewing area into the room itself, but this encourages the impression that the assistant is doing some kind of unseen work, behind the mirror. Because the goal is to minimize the attention that the participants pay to the mirror and whatever may be happening behind it, separate entrances are the preferred design.

In addition to these standard features, professional focus group facilities may include any number of high-tech options. The discussion above on video has already alluded to the possibility of remote viewing. Some facilities in fact offer remote video hook-ups, so that the observers can be at multiple locations throughout the world. Within the facility itself, there may electronic provisions for communications between the observers and the moderator during the group itself, such as through a "bug in the ear" or a small computer monitor that is mounted below the tabletop, out of sight of the participants. Many facilities can also provide the participants with electronic connections for "perception analyzers," "response meters," and other devices for collecting feedback during the discussion.

Focus Groups in Private Homes

In the United States, it is far more common to hold focus groups in either an adapted conference room or a professional facility than in someone's home. This is not necessarily the case in other countries, however. For example, in Great Britain, "living room" focus groups are more common. One of the best-known British uses of private homes for focus groups came from studies of how ordinary viewers react to television programs, including the nightly news. By first gathering people to watch a program and then leading a discussion afterwards, this approach has a strong linkage to some of the earliest uses of focus groups in getting immediate responses to live radio broadcasts.

The most common way to arrange a focus group in a private home is to start by locating the person who will host the group at his or her home. This host will also typically serve as the nucleus of the recruitment efforts. In essence, the recruitment is a form of "snowball sampling" that invites neighbors and friends to spend an evening at the host's house. Although any one participant may not know all of the others, all will be mutual acquaintances of the host. In some cases, the hosts may volunteer their efforts as a contribution to the project; more commonly, they are paid for their work. Readers who are familiar with selling housewares through parties or political fund-raising coffees will recognize the same basic strategy here.

The research team usually works with the host, both to determine the guest list and to make the in-home arrangements. Often, the guest list will incorporate some screening criteria in order to ensure the compatibility of the participants and to create segmentation across the different groups. For example, one set of hosts may be bringing together people in blue-collar neighborhoods, while another set of hosts come from upper-middle-income neighborhoods.

The physical arrangements for conducting a focus group in a living room are, of course, quite unpredictable. There is no requirement that the group actually be held in the living room. If the participants need to do some writing or if you want them all gathered in a face-to-face setting, a dining room table or equivalent may be preferable. Whatever the location, it needs to be compatible with the research team's audiotaping requirements. Needless to say, videotaping is rare in this environment.

The Focus Group Guidebook **Has a Brief History of Focus Groups**

Researchers who are interested in political issues have made the most use of focus groups in private homes. For example, television news reporters sometimes bring people together in a private home to provide instant feedback after watching a presidential debate.

Political sociologist William Gamson provides a more serious example of using living-room focus groups to discuss political issues. His study created more than 30 groups of four to six "working people" to talk about the issues of affirmative action, nuclear power, troubled industry, and the Arab-Israeli conflict. The goal was to encourage these acquaintances to share a conversation on each of these issues. To maximize compa-

EXAMPLE

Talking Politics

rability across the groups, the moderators followed a set script, but they minimized their participation in the groups themselves. In addition, to help focus the conversation, the moderators passed around "stimulus material" in the form of political cartoons related to each issue.

In a similar study, Theodore Sasson brought together neighbors throughout the Boston area to discuss their ideas about crime. While Gamson used a wide range of sources to locate the hosts for his focus groups, Sasson contacted members of each local crime watch group to locate individuals who would be willing to host this discussion. Building on preexisting ties to the research topic is thus a useful way to overcome one of the major obstacles to holding focus groups in private homes: locating the hosts. (Gamson, 1992; Sasson, 1995)

At Any Location, Consider Food

Food can really help focus groups, since eating together tends to promote conversation and communication within the group. Most focus groups use a variety of snacks, such as cookies or pastries, but full meals also can be effective. Snacks and light refreshments are typically placed on a table to one side of the room and are enjoyed at the beginning of the focus group, during the presession small talk.

What kinds of snacks work best?

- Chocolate-chip cookies are favorites, especially if they are high quality.
- Popcorn tastes great and avoids the crunchy sound of some other snacks.
- Small pieces of fresh fruit and vegetables provide nice variety.

With full meals, consider having the food catered or delivered. If you are doing focus groups on a regular basis, it helps to develop a relationship with a good catering service that understands your needs. If you are just providing a simple meal, either a box lunch or a deli-tray buffet is a good option. For younger participants, pizza is the most common choice.

When you are serving a full meal, remember that individuals' dietary needs and preferences vary. The best way to deal with this issue is to inquire about it during the recruitment contact.

When the meal is being provided by a restaurant at the group site, make sure that the arrangements are established well in advance, so the kitchen staff knows when to prepare the food. One common arrangement is to provide a light snack before the group and the main meal afterwards. Otherwise, if the meal comes first, it may be hard to keep the participants from discussing the topic before the group starts.

Whatever meal you are serving, plan ahead to keep the noise level down. With snacks, many of the bagged items, such as potato chips and corn chips, can be quite noisy. With a full meal, eating during the taping will almost certainly affect your ability to hear or understand what is being said. Meals that involve china, glassware, and silver add to the noise level. Pouring water is a particular problem, since it tends to mask the sound frequencies of the human voice, so keep water pitchers and other beverages on a side table.

11

Checklist for Planning Focus Groups

General Planning

- Define the purpose and outcomes of the project.
- Identify personnel and budgetary resources.
- Develop the timeline for the project.
- Decide how structured the groups will be.
- Decide who the participants will be.
- Write the questions for the interview guide (questioning route).
- Decide how large the groups will be.
- Decide how many groups there will be.
- Choose the locations, dates, and times for the sessions.

Planning Related to Recruitment

- Identify the appropriate composition for each group.
- Determine the source(s) for recruitment contacts.

- Develop eligibility and exclusion criteria for individual participants.
- Develop recruitment screening and contact scripts.
- Determine the follow-up procedures that will ensure attendance.

Planning Related to Moderating

- Define the role of the moderator.
- Select or train skilled moderators.
- Create external props or stimulus materials to be used in the sessions.

Planning Related to Analysis

- Design the analysis plan.
- Specify the elements of the final report.
- Define data to be generated: field notes, tapes, transcripts, and so on.
- Clarify the sponsor's involvement at the focus group sessions.

References

Gamson, W. (1992). *Talking politics*. New York: Cambridge University Press.

Glaser, B., & Strauss, A. (1967). *The discovery of grounded theory*. New York: Aldine de Gruyter.

Kitzinger, J. (1994). The methodology of focus groups: The importance of interaction between research participants. *Sociology of Health and Illness, 16,* 103-121.

Sasson, T. (1995). *Crime talk*. New York: Aldine de Gruyter.

Index to
This Volume

Index to the
Focus Group Kit

The letter preceding the page number refers to the volume, according to the following key:

About the Author

David L. Morgan received his Ph.D. in sociology from the University of Michigan and did post-doctoral work at Indiana University. He is currently a professor in the Institute on Aging at Portland State University's College of Urban and Public Affairs. In addition to his continuing work with focus groups, he has a wide-ranging interest in research methods, including designs that combine qualitative and quantitative methods.  Within gerontology, his research interests center on the aging of the baby boomers—a topic that should keep him busy until his own retirement!

Notes

Notes

Notes

Notes

Notes